Under the Mulberry Tree

Book Three
Jacob's Daughter series

WRITTEN BY

Samantha Jillian Bayarr

PRINTED IN THE UNITED STATES

Samantha Jillian Bayarr
Book THREE of Jacob's Daughter series

Also by Samantha Jillian Bayarr

LWF Amish Series
Little Wild Flower Book I
Little Wild Flower Book II
The Taming of a Wild Flower
Little Wild Flower in Bloom
Little Wild Flower's Journey

Christian Romance
Milk Maid in Heaven
The Anniversary

Christian Historical Romance
A Sheriff's Legacy: Book One
Preacher Outlaw: Book Two
Cattle Rustler in Petticoats: Book Three

Jacob's Daughter Amish Collection
Jacob's Daughter
Amish Winter Wonderland
Under the Mulberry Tree
Amish Winter of Promises
Chasing Fireflies
Amish Summer of Courage
An Amish Harvest
An Amish Christmas Wish

Companion Series
An Amish Courtship
The Quilter's Son
An Amish Widower
Amish Sisters

Chapter 1

"What do you mean he's not my real father?"

Abby was shaking, while aiming imaginary daggers at her *mamm.*

Lizzie reached out to her *dochder,* but when Abby flinched away, she slowly retracted her hand.

Abby stood up from the porch swing abruptly and stood near the railing. A slight wind blew stray hairs from beneath her prayer *kapp,* which she angrily pushed behind her ear. The warm October sun shone brightly on her cheeks, heating her almost to agitation, but she wouldn't turn to face her *mamm.*

Abby picked at splattered vegetables on her apron, silence weighing heavily between her and her *mamm.* If only she hadn't confided in her *mamm* about the teasing from her peers about Jonah Beiler, whom she just realized was not really her cousin.

They'd spent most of the day at a canning bee, and the *menner* had been there to help bring in the bushels of fruits and vegetables for canning. At the noon meal, she'd sat with the youth until her cousin, Jonah, decided to tell the others about their beautiful, forbidden kiss under the mulberry tree in the school yard. No one had seen them do it, and they'd made a pact that it would never happen again. But there he sat, betraying her confidence.

Before she realized, everyone was calling them *kissing cousins.* Abby couldn't take it anymore and left the Miller's *haus.* When her *mamm* caught up to her later at home, Abby had no choice but to tell her about what happened, but denied the kiss ever happened. If only it had been that easy for her or her *mamm* to tell the truth. Then none of this would have mattered. Her love for Jonah would not have felt like a sin, and her peers would never have teased her since she and Jonah were not blood-related after all.

Abby swung around angrily. "How could you have lied to me my entire life? I'm almost twenty years old; you could have told me a long time ago and spared me and everyone else a lot of trouble. Does *Daed*...I mean, *Jacob,* know about this, or did you lie to him too?"

Lizzie sighed. "Yes, he knows, Abby, but you have to understand *why* I lied."

"There is *never* any reason to tell a lie this big! Who is it *Mother?* Who is my real father? And why have you kept him from me all these years?"

Lizzie tried to remain calm. "Do you remember why we moved here?"

Abby rolled her eyes. "Of course I do. Because that guy Eddie was after us…oh heavens no…*please* tell me my real father is *not* Eddie the drug addict!"

Lizzie's face drained of all color except for the blazing red of her cheeks. "I'm sorry, Abby, but it's true."

Abby couldn't breathe. Her whole life had been a lie. She was the child of a drug addict—a man who was dead. Tears pooled in her eyes as she stared down the long drive that led to the main road. The wind blew orange and red leaves across the lawn. Even they had purpose. As for her, she no longer had a father.

Abby brushed past her *mamm* and into the *haus*. She took the stairs two at a time until she reached the top.

In her room, she pushed on her heavy bureau, determined to block the door that had no lock. The feet of the large piece of furniture dug into the hardwood floor, but she finally wedged it in front of the door. Then she threw herself onto her bed, and began to sob into the quilt she and her *mamm* had made together.

A light knock sounded at the door.

Abby turned slightly. "Go away *mother.* I'll never believe another word that comes from your mouth!"

Abby quieted her sobbing long enough to listen to the fading footfalls of her *mamm,* letting her know that she'd given up the fight.

She slid down from the bed onto the floor, where she retrieved the small suitcase from under her bed that she'd brought with her when she and her *mamm* had come to the community. Tossing it up on the bed, she filled it with her few belongings, including the two thousand dollars she'd saved from working for her *aenti* Lillian at the bakery. Picking up the packed suitcase, Abby crossed the room and pushed open her window and tossed the suitcase out the window, watching mindlessly as it hit the front lawn below.

Pushing the bureau back in the corner of her room, she ran down the stairs and out the front door, her *mamm* fast on her heels.

"Abby, *kume* sit back and down and talk to me."

Abby turned; her face flush. "I don't want to hear another word that comes from your mouth ever again. I'm leaving here and never coming back. There is nothing for me here but a life full of lies. *"*

Her last words to her *mamm* had stung them both that day, and Abby had not been able to remove them, or the look on her *mamm's* face from her memory since the day she spoke them five long years before.

Chapter 2

FIVE YEARS LATER…

Stepping off the bus, Abby wondered if she'd really gotten all the rebellion out of her system after spending the last five years among the *Englischers,* and if she was really ready to return home and make amends with her *mamm.* Her *mamm's* reaction to her return would determine if she was truly ready to be baptized into the church and make a life for herself in the Amish community.

Now, at nearly twenty-five years old, she knew it would be tough to go back, and the possibility of running into Jonah Beiler after all this time would be even tougher. Over the years, she'd had time to get over his admission about kissing her under the mulberry tree, but the embarrassment had made her swear off boys forever.

Jonah had made a career out of teasing her, and up until the point where he told everyone about the their shared kiss, the worst thing he'd ever said about her was that she'd kissed a frog down at Goose Pond when she hadn't. She was sure Jonah had no idea the impact his lie that day would have on her entire life, but that didn't make it any easier to forgive him. Jonah was three years older than Abby, and she felt he should know better than to do such a thing. Even now, she feared they would forever be branded as *kissing cousins*.

Jonah had been a thorn in her side from the moment they'd first met—always teasing her and getting her into trouble. But as the years passed, they became closer. And when Abby turned eighteen, their relationship changed entirely. They started to develop feelings for each other that others might consider an unholy crush. It wasn't until she went home and complained to her *mamm* about the youth teasing her, that she discovered the truth. The full impact of her *mamm*'s lie had changed her entire life.

But that was in the past, and she was prepared to make amends with everyone—even Jonah. As for his *schweschder,* Becca, she'd missed her wedding to Levi Graber. Abby and Becca had been best friends, in addition to their supposed blood-relation to one another. There was a lot of lost time she needed to make up for with her friend, and she hoped the time had not caused a break in their friendship.

There were a number of different reasons Abby left that day, her *mamm's* lies being at the top of that list. If the truth be told, the idea had been building in Abby ever since she and her *mamm* had first stepped foot onto Amish soil. She'd been trying to break free, always feeling a nagging in the back of her mind that she didn't fit in. When she discovered why, suddenly everything made perfect sense. The breaking point for Abby began with her love for Jonah Beiler, and ended with her *mamm's* lies. Those lies had torn her away from the only father she'd ever known, and from Jonah, who could have been her husband had she known it was not a sin to love him.

Her decision to leave the community stemmed more from her desire to escape the life she'd felt trapped in for the previous nine years. She loved her parents, but when she discovered that Jacob Yoder was not her real father, she no longer needed an excuse to leave; it was already well-formed in her mind. She'd felt betrayed by her *mamm*, and she pitied Jacob for accepting the responsibility of raising her when he knew he couldn't possibly be her real father. Finding out she was really half *Englisch* was enough to make her want to revisit her past.

The fight between her and her *mamm* escalated to beyond reason and had prompted her to do the very same thing her *mamm* had done when she was about the same age—run.

But here she was, about to walk back into the Amish community that had claimed her childhood. The only difference between her return and that of her *mamm*, was that she wasn't toting a child along with her.

After leaving home, she'd gone back to the same small town where she'd spent the first ten years of her life, and had worked at The Brick Oven, a large bakery in the historic district downtown. Having developed a love and obvious talent for creating Amish pastries and pies that drew in customers for miles, Abby's confections kept the bakery from going under in a weak economy. She hadn't planned on returning to Ohio, but she'd missed the friends she'd left behind as a child, and wanted to revisit the childhood memories. But they hadn't quite turned out to be what she'd remembered them to be.

The home they'd lived in was now run-down and in a bad part of town. Maybe it had always been that way, but she'd thought things differently as a child. She hadn't even meant to stay for so long in the battered town, but when she landed the job at the bakery, time stood still. For the first time, she felt she had something that was hers alone. Then she reunited with her best friend, Rachel. They'd become roommates and had a lot of fun together—in the beginning.

When Rachel began to bring home boyfriends to spend the night, Abby pulled away from her and began working more hours at the bakery, much to her employer's delight. She loved making Amish treats that customers would line up out the door just to get a taste of. There were always several standing orders every day from her regular customers who had come to depend on her sweet creations to keep them satisfied.

But when the letter came from *Onkel* Seth explaining the hardship he and *Aenti* Lillian had endured, she couldn't turn down his plea asking for help with the bakery. At that point, Abby knew it was time go home to her *familye* in Indiana; no matter how much she dreaded facing her *mamm,* she couldn't pass up the opportunity to go home to the Amish community where she knew in her heart, she belonged.

While in Ohio, she'd managed to find Eddie's older sister, and his parents. It was nice to find *familye* she hadn't known she had, but it just wasn't the same. True, she'd adapted to life in the Amish community and had accepted Jacob as her *daed,* but having blood relatives in Ohio seemed to make a difference—in the beginning. Still, she felt alone there, and lacked a true sense of belonging. The only place she'd felt completely accepted was at home in Indiana with her *mamm* and Jacob—her *daed.*

Chapter 3

Abby felt overwhelmed as she pulled her suitcase behind her across the bus depot—until her eyes locked onto the last person she expected to see.

"*Daed.* I'm so glad to see you.*"*

Abby threw her arms around the aging man, a sense of home claiming her emotions.

"I'll always be your *daed,*" Jacob whispered.

Abby pulled away, wishing she'd worn the plain dress she'd left home in, instead of the *Englisch* clothing. She wrapped her coat around her, trying to hide her attire as she searched her *daed's* face for acceptance. Abby felt he looked older than she'd remembered, and his eyes held sadness behind the smile he so desperately clung to. His hair and beard had thinned, and both were peppered with more gray than the last time she'd seen him. She suddenly felt responsible for the crease in his brow that suggested more worry than she cared to see, but his welcoming nature would never let her take the blame. Still, she felt suddenly very selfish for leaving without telling him goodbye when she'd run off five years ago.

"I'm so sorry I left, *Daed.* How's *Mamm?"*

His smile widened. "She's eager to see you. Let's get you home where you belong."

Home. Could it really be that easy?

Jacob picked up his *dochder's Englisch* suitcase, looking past the blue jeans and form-fitting shirt she wore, and tossed it in the back of the buggy.

At least she hasn't cut her hair.

Abby climbed into the buggy feeling a little strange sitting next to her *daed,* as it was apparent to anyone looking at him that he was Amish. She, for all anyone knew, was an *Englischer.* Her feelings were conflicted at the moment, but she intended to honor her parents by dressing Amish while back at home. The problem was, she didn't *feel* very Amish at the moment. Before she left the community, she'd stopped questioning who she was, but when her *mamm* told her the truth about Jacob, she suddenly felt lost in her place in the community and didn't feel she could stay there. But could she go home now and put it all behind her? She wasn't sure of much at the moment, except she wanted to try—for the sake of her *familye*.

They rode in silence, leaving too much time for thoughts of regret to seep into Abby's mind. She had tried to push back the guilt about running from her *familye* for nearly five years, and now it was rushing back in a sea of bad memories and last words. She and her *mamm* had written to each other over the years, but they'd managed to avoid talking about that final day when everything escalated

She knew now what she didn't know then—that her *mamm's* lies were only to protect her from a dangerous *mann* who had less paternal love for her than the ground she walked on. God's green earth was far kinder to her than her biological father had been capable of, and she felt bad that it had taken her so long to realize it. The land and the community that resided in it were all that she needed.

Her *familye* had taught her to appreciate that such simple things were the very core of who she was, and trying to find herself among the *Englisch* would never fill her heart the way home could.

Abby knew she had a lot of fences to mend, and she had to start with the *mann* sitting quietly beside her.

"I was surprised to see you at the bus depot—especially after I never even said "goodbye" to you when I left. I'm sorry for acting so immature. I love you, *Daed.* I hope you know that."

Jacob clicked at the mare, steering her off the main road. "Abby, there is no reason to bring up the past when it's been forgiven. You're home now, and that's all that matters."

Abby shifted nervously in her seat. "I want you to know that I'm home to stay."

Jacob kept his eyes on the road. "I'm glad to hear that. So you'll be taking the baptism then?"

She didn't need to wait for her *mamm's* approval of her return. Having her *dead* pick her up was confirmation enough for Abby. "*Jah*. I'd like to go see Bishop Troyer first thing tomorrow morning. Will you drive me?"

The corners of Jacob's mouth turned up into a smile. "I think that's a *gut* idea, but let's get you home first; your *mamm* has been waiting a long time to see you."

The mare increased speed as they pulled onto the long drive to the *haus*. The horse knew she was home, even if Abby didn't. Despite the familiar row of snow-laden oak trees lining the lane, and the icy pond, it was difficult for Abby's heart to accept. Anticipation and dread filled her entire being at the thought of seeing her *mamm* again.

Chapter 4

Abby stepped down from buggy in front of the *haus,* and stood there while Jacob put away the horse. She willed her feet to move, but she couldn't get them past the freshly shoveled walkway that led to the snow-covered porch. Abby listened to the wind push at the porch swing, weighed down with snow, the rusted chain squeaking in protest. Remembering how the sound used to comfort her, she shuffled her feet toward the steps, hoping her wobbly legs would support her effort to reach the front door.

The familiar sound of the door hinge made her look up in time to meet her *mamm's* soulful eyes. Her *mamm* knew the difficulty Abby faced without even having to say a word. She, herself, was the prodigal son in female form, and she, too, had come home looking for redemption.

Tears pooled in Lizzie's eyes and her heart beat out of sync at the sight of her *dochder*. Despite the *Englisch* clothes, and the long hair cascading from beneath her pink, knitted hat, Lizzie could still see her *dochder* beneath all of it.

She didn't wait for an invitation. She hurried down the porch steps and pulled Abby close, taking in the smell of her grown up *boppli*. How she'd missed that smell of baking spices that had clung to Abby from the day she'd made her first snitz pie. It was the scent only a mother could love, and she'd longed for it for too long.

Abby succumbed to her *mamm's* embrace that felt like a cool breeze on a hot day, quenching a need that brought relief to her very soul. All thoughts of the past dwindled away in that one embrace, leaving her wondering why she'd ever left home in the first place. She felt suddenly very safe and protected like a baby chick under its momma's wing. It was a feeling she never wanted to lose again.

"I missed you so much, *Mamm*. I'm so sorry for leaving the way I did. Please forgive me for breaking your heart."

Lizzie kissed her *dochder's* hair. "I'm the one who needs forgiveness. I promise I will never tell another lie as long as I live."

Abby sighed, her warm breath creating a vapor into the cold air. "Let's go inside where it's warm. I could use a cup of your hot cocoa with a dollop of whipped cream and cinnamon on top."

Lizzie smiled. "That's a *gut* idea. And we'll make some for your *daed*—I mean, Jacob."

Abby turned to her *mamm,* a serious expression clouding her face. "He's my *daed.*"

Lizzie's eyes moistened with tears again. "You know he loves you like you were his own *dochder.*"

Abby nodded. "I *am* his *dochder.* I know that now.*"

Nothing more needed to be said about it. They both knew where the other stood on the matter, and for once, they both agreed.

Abby ran a hand along the handmade quilt she and her *mamm* had made at one of the quilting bees when they'd first arrived in the community fifteen years ago. She recalled the feel of the gathering that had welcomed them, and worked hard to provide her *mamm* with a belated wedding dowry after she'd married Jacob—her *daed.* Funny how that word no longer felt foreign to her the way it had for so long after she'd run off.

Abby examined more closely the squares of fabric she'd stitched, noting the difference in the quality versus that of her *mamm.* Remembering the stories told to her about her *grossmammi* attending quilting bees with her *mamm* at the same age brought a lump to her throat. There were many times over the past five years that Abby had wished she'd taken the quilt with her. None of that mattered now. She was finally home to stay.

Hoisting her suitcase up onto her childhood bed, she determined to unpack only the necessities and leave the rest in there. She would store it under the bed until she could figure out what to do with the *Englisch* clothes it contained. From a set of hooks near the door, she lifted a purple dress. The material was freshly ironed, and it smelled of winter air. She was certain her *mamm* had hung it on the outside line in anticipation of her homecoming. She always loved the smell of clothes drying outside—even in winter, and her *mamm* had made it even more welcoming.

Pulling the freshly laundered dress over her head, she was reminded of the first time she put on a plain dress. She had made such a fuss with her *mamm* that day, fighting with her and complaining. She wondered if it would have made a difference if she'd learned the truth back then. It was very possible that they would have never come to live in the community, and she would never have known Jacob as the loving *daed* that he is. Abby had been the most unfair to him when she'd left home, and her siblings—especially Caleb, had taken her sudden disappearance very hard.

After stuffing the suitcase under the bed, Abby walked toward the door to exit the room. The tell-tale squeak of the loose floorboard caused her heart to quicken. Pausing, she toyed with her emotions over the contents of the small space beneath the floorboard that held her hidden treasures away from the rest of the world. Unable to resist a small peek, she knelt down and pulled back the braided rug. Sticking her finger into the small knothole, she yanked on the resistant board until it gave way. She sat on her haunches and stared into the rectangular opening for the longest time, savoring the contents as if they were relished jewels.

Blowing the dust from the opening, she lifted the Hello Kitty shirt from its neatly folded state and held it up for examination. Her *mamm's* cell phone lay at the bottom as evidence of a lie that Abby had told regarding its whereabouts. The items were, at the age of ten, her last links to the *Englisch* world she'd left behind. The only value they held now was to serve as proof of a life better left behind.

Chapter 5

In the kitchen, Abby found her only *schweschder,* Rachel, helping her *mamm* with the evening meal. At nearly fifteen, it was apparent that Rachel was a lot more comfortable in the kitchen than Abby had been at that age. Awkwardness claimed Abby as she looked for an opportunity to blend with her *mamm's* and Rachel's routine. Taking a deep breath, Abby stepped in and pulled the dishes from the shelf to set the table. She knew if she didn't take charge of the situation, her younger sibling would never respect her, and would more than likely treat her as an outsider.

"*Denki, Mamm,* for washing my dresses and hanging them outside to dry. They smell *wunderbaar.*"

Lizzie smiled at her *dochder.* "I wanted you to feel at home."

Abby looked at her *mamm* thoughtfully. "I do. How are *Onkel* Seth and *Aenti* Lillian? I'm eager to see them Sunday at church service."

Lizzie's eyes showed stress at the mention of her *bruder* and his *fraa*. "They weren't in attendance at the service two weeks ago, and when we tried to visit, Lillian wouldn't get out of bed to greet us. She didn't even want to attend the *boppli's* funeral, but my *bruder* enforced it. Did your *onkel* tell you they had to do emergency surgery at the hospital to remove her uterus? She nearly bled to death, and my *bruder* would have been burying her too. The *boppli* was stillborn; there was nothing they could do to save him."

Tears choked Abby. Her *onkel* hadn't said any of that in his brief letter to her—but how could he? No wonder he needed someone to take over the bakery.

"Can we try to visit Sunday after the service?"

Lizzie forced a smile. "We can always try. I'm sure she'd be happy to see you."

Abby breathed a silent prayer for her *aenti.* She felt guilty for not being there for her *aenti* in her time of need. Lillian was one more person with whom Abby had a lot of making up to do.

Jonah pushed open the large, double doors of the oversized barn in which he built buggies. The cold night air welcomed him after a long day of work, and his empty stomach alerted him he'd missed another meal. He looked toward the end of his property where the Miller's bakery sat closed, just as it had for over a month. When Seth had told him he'd sent for Abby's return so she could run the bakery in his *fraa's* absence, Jonah had mixed feelings about the situation. Though his stomach would be happy to have fresh baked goods from the bakery, he was a little more than apprehensive about seeing Abby again.

Jonah made his way through the deep snow to the small *haus* he'd built on the property he'd acquired a year ago from Efram Stoltzfus. Since Lillian and Seth had set up *haus* at Hiram Miller's farm after they married, Jonah had been able to purchase all but the small lot where Lillian's bakery had stood. Jonah was happy to purchase the land, as he wanted to expand on his buggy making business. After his *daed's* death, Jonah gave the *haus* to his newlywed *schweschder* since they'd wanted a bigger place to raise a family. The vacant land Jonah purchased had originally been for Lillian's dowry, but Seth's unwillingness to leave his *daed* had turned into an opportunity for Jonah.

Come Monday, Jonah knew he would have to be on his guard around Abby, fearing his sinful feelings for his cousin would return. After Abby had left the community, he'd had to confess to the Bishop and take the sole responsibility for their error in judgment regarding the forbidden kiss.

Though Jonah knew his sweet tooth would probably draw him to the bakery again, he would need to keep his distance from Abby, especially with how vulnerable he'd felt when he learned of her return to the community.

He'd felt responsible for her hasty departure, despite her *mamm* telling him it was something Abby just needed to get "out of her system". He couldn't help but wonder if her reaction to breaking her trust that last day he'd seen her had everything to do with her decision to leave. Despite all the praying and confessing to *Gott* over his love for Abby, he felt the worst over hurting her with his foolish betrayal.

Jonah was determined to keep his feelings in check, and to make sure he didn't hurt Abby again—even if that meant staying away from the bakery. It would be tough to do since the bakery sat at the edge of his property, and he would have to drive by whenever he went anywhere. He couldn't avoid her indefinitely—not that he wanted to.

Abby cuddled up in the warm quilt that smelled like winter sunshine. She was exhausted, but sleep eluded her. She would be baptized tomorrow, putting to rest the *Englisch* part of her. Having spent the past five years among the *Englisch,* she knew there was nothing there for her. Despite having Eddie's family; her true *familye* bonds were here in the Amish community. The odds of finding a suitable mate in either community were against her, but she was determined to devote herself to *familye.*

A light knock interrupted her reverie.

"Are you awake?" Rachel's whisper was barely audible, but the quietness of the *haus* allowed her voice to permeate the barrier between them.

Abby sat up, noting the bright moonlight streaming in through her window. "*Jah. Kume.*"

Rachel opened the door slowly, and stood quietly in the doorway. Abby patted the edge of her bed, beckoning her *schweschder* to sit with her. With downcast eyes, Rachel walked timidly toward the bed and lowered herself cautiously to the edge.

Abby slipped the corner of quilt around the shivering child. "It's very cold tonight, *jah?*"

Rachel leaned back and cradled the spare pillow under her arm, leaning on one elbow to face Abby.

"I'm glad you're home because now I will have someone to tell all my secrets to."

Shocked at the strange turnaround in her *schweschder's* attitude, Abby leaned on her elbow facing Rachel, eager to listen to all she had to say.

Chapter 6

Despite the cold snow blowing into the buggy, Abby's hands and neck were on fire and damp with sweat. Was it too late to rethink the decision to get baptized? She'd prayed about it late into the night after Rachel had finally gone back to her own bed. Her *schweschder's* words kept ringing in her ears, leaving her wondering what the community would think of her return. Her *bruder,* Caleb still hadn't spoken a word to her, but thanks to Rachel's secrets, Abby knew why.

It was no secret to Abby that Caleb was bothered by her hasty departure, and her return that echoed the same. But nothing had prepared her to hear from Rachel that Caleb had tried to convince her *familye* to shun her after she'd left the community.

The few letters she'd received from her *mamm* while she was away had hinted that Caleb had not approved of her actions. Since no one else was home the day she left, Lizzie had kept the truth from the *kinner,* confiding only in her husband, who knew the circumstances. Abby would have preferred the truth to be out in the open, but it wasn't her story to tell—it was her parent's story.

Another thought pricked Abby's heart. How was she to fully confess to the Bishop and accept her baptism if she wasn't able to explain her extended absence from the community without betraying her *mamm?* She couldn't. The only way to handle it was to take full responsibility for leaving, and keep her *mamm's* lie out of it. It wasn't her lie to tell, and it would have no bearing on her confession. In her heart, this was what she wanted to do more than anything—to be baptized and remain in the community. Being free from her *mamm's* secrets and lies would make it a lot easier.

At dinner, Abby was surprised when Caleb asked her to get him another slice of pie. She wasn't sure if it was for the sake of the *familye* that he'd spoken, or because she had received the baptism, but she was about to find out.

Caleb pushed his chair back from the table and locked his eyes on Abby. "May I have a word with you out in the barn?"

Abby looked to her *mamm* with pleading eyes.

Lizzie shooed her *dochder* with her hand. "Go on now and talk to your *bruder* while I take care of the dishes."

For the first time in five years, it hit her that Caleb wasn't her *bruder* after all, and it felt foreign to hear her *mamm* say it. She paused, but when her *mamm* reminded her to put on her coat, she snapped out of her conflicting thoughts.

Caleb turned on the gas lights that hung from the rafters of barn, and closed the door against the snow.

"I brought you out here because I didn't think Rachel and Liam needed to hear what I wanted to say to you."

Abby looked at him sternly. "Rachel told me you wanted the *familye* to shun me after I left five years ago."

Caleb busied himself by picking up a broom and sweeping the already clean floor between the stalls. "If you hadn't taken the baptism today, I would have insisted on it. When you first came to live with us, I was too young to understand the impact it would have in my life to have an *Englischer* as a *schweschder"*

Does he know we're not related?

"At the time, all I cared about was having a new *mamm,* and I admit, she's been very *gut* to me and to my *daed.* But if you are going to reside here, you need to get rid of the *Englisch* clothes and the *Englisch* ways. Put it all behind you because I don't want you to influence our *bruder* and *schweschder* negatively."

Abby put her hands on her hips. "The last time I checked , *Daed* was the head of this *familye,* not you. And this is *my familye* too, not just yours."

"For the last five years you have not shown that they're your *familye.* What of that?"

Abby started to walk away and then turned abruptly. "I don't have to put up with you talking to me. You aren't even…"

Abby bit her tongue. She couldn't finish her sentence without exposing her parent's lies to Caleb, who seemed oblivious to the truth. He wasn't her *bruder,* but she wouldn't hurt him with the truth, no matter how unfair he was being toward her.

"We're grown up now, Abby, and we're going to have to learn to treat each other as adults. We only had a few years together as children, and now we must put our grownup troubles behind us for the sake of the *familye.* "

Abby swallowed the tears that tried to make their way from her throat to her eyes. She wasn't the only one that had been hurt by the lie that her *mamm* and *daed* had chosen to keep hidden.

"I'm here to stay, dear *bruder.* I'm sorry if my actions hurt you or the rest of the *familye.* I won't give you any cause for concern. My loyalties are to this *familye* from here on out."

Caleb's look softened. He reached for Abby, and she allowed him to tuck her under the comfort of his arm as they walked out of the barn. "I missed you, Abby."

Chapter 7

Abby looked out her bedroom window at the fresh blanket of snow that covered the ground, and caused a white shadow to form along the tree branches. From this view, with the sun barely peeking over the horizon, her world seemed serene and without problems. She silently thanked *Gott* for the chance to make a fresh start in the community, and for the strength to overcome her fears of attending her first church service.

Abby chose a dark pink dress for the service. Though she knew she needed to put aside any residual feelings she may have for Jonah, she couldn't help but wonder if he'd thought of her over the past five years. It was foolish for her to hope that they could ever have a future together, given that the entire community, including Jonah, believed them to be first cousins. She was determined to keep busy with the bakery—anything to take her mind off Jonah. That wouldn't be an easy task. After all, a girl never forgets her first love—she carries it with her all her life.

If it be Your wille, Gotte, please bless me with a husband. Please help me to forget Jonah.

Jonah fidgeted with his hat as he walked into the Graber home just before the service began. Deciding he didn't want the temptation to see Abby during the service, he took a seat on the end of the front bench.

Within minutes, Caleb pushed his way onto the bench next to him. "Why are you sitting way up here this morning?"

Jonah cleared his throat. "Just felt like a change is all."

Caleb nudged him. "You know Abby's back."

"*Jah,* I heard. You never mention she was coming back. Didn't you know either?"

Caleb picked up the *Ausbund* from the bench beside him and opened it to the first hymn. "*Jah,* I knew about it, but I didn't say anything because I didn't think she would really come back, much less get baptized yesterday."

Jonah raised an eyebrow. "She was baptized yesterday?"

"*Jah*, I was surprised too. But if she intended to live in our *haus,* she needed to make her commitment to *Gott* and the community."

The singing of the hymn began, and Jonah found it hard to concentrate enough to sing along. Since Abby had taken the baptism, that would mean she would remain in the community. How was he going to avoid her? Did he even feel the same for her?

It doesn't matter. My love for her is forbidden. Please Gott, help me to forget Abby, and send me a fraa.

As the service neared its end, Abby left her seat beside Rachel and went into the kitchen to help the women set out the food for the shared meal. She'd noticed her *bruder* sitting with a handsome *mann* at the front of the room, and hoped he would introduce her. Knowing the *mann* was single from his lack of a beard, she hoped to make a good impression in case he wasn't betrothed. Maybe there was hope for her to find a husband in the community after all.

Before long, Abby was so busy serving the *menner,* that she didn't notice Caleb when he walked up in front of her. Her *bruder's* friend had her back to them, but when he turned around, Abby nearly dropped the plate of food she had extended to Caleb.

It was Jonah—no mistake about it.

Abby allowed herself to peruse his physique, noting that he'd outgrown his skinny youth. He was now slim, but strong; the outline of his chest and arms showed muscle that he never had before. She liked it. When she finally gazed into his eyes, her pulse raced, as she lost herself in their blue depths, just as she had many times as a teenager. She wanted to throw her arms around him and tell him how much she'd missed him, but she couldn't. Giddiness rushed through her as he smiled at her.

Jonah's eyes darted nervously between Caleb and Abby, who seemed to be shocked to see him. But when his eyes locked with hers, he saw a familiarity that made him swoon all over again. If it was possible, she was more beautiful than he'd remembered. Her hazel eyes were welcoming, her milky skin accented by the flattering blush of her cheeks. More than ever, he wanted to pull her into his arms and declare his love for her, but it was forbidden. There was no denying he still loved her, but he had to keep it buried, for the community would not allow a marriage between first cousins any more than the *Englischers* would.

Abby shook herself from her reverie. "Jonah, it's so *gut* to see you again."

Jonah nodded nervously. "*Jah.* It's been a long time—five years?"

Abby cast her eyes downward. "*Jah.* It's been too long. But I'm back now—to stay. I was baptized yesterday."

Jonah wasn't sure if he was happy about that or not. "*Jah,* your *bruder* told me. *Das gut.* Welcome back, cousin."

The words stung Abby. She wanted to scream out that she wasn't his cousin—that she loved him—still. Timidity and propriety were taught among the community, but she almost didn't care if she broke the rules. She wanted Jonah to know they weren't cousins. But she couldn't do that without dishonoring her *mamm* and *daed.*

"Denki, Cousin." Abby nearly choked on the words, but they needed to be said. For the sake of having them sink in, if for nothing else.

Chapter 8

Jacob pulled the family buggy into his *bruder*-in law's yard. After assisting Lizzie out of the buggy, he offered the same to his *kinner,* but they all bound out like white rabbits hopping in the deep snow. All except for Abby, who lingered in the back, seemingly lost in thought.

Jacob reached for her. "Abby, *kume.* I thought you were eager to see your *onkel* Seth and *Aenti* Lillian."

Abby looked at her *daed* quizzically. How long had she been sitting there daydreaming of Jonah? Was it possible her *daed* could tell what she was thinking about?

Abby dipped her head, hoping he wouldn't see her flaming cheeks, and took the hand he extended to her. Pushing the lap quilt aside, she stepped from the buggy into the deep snow, wishing she'd worn her boots instead of her brown loafers. She had decided on them when they left the *haus* a few hours ago, thinking they would look nicer with her dress. Now, she was paying for such thoughts of vanity with cold, wet feet.

Inside, *Onkel* Seth scrambled to push open the draperies on the windows to let the bright sun into the rooms that seemed lifeless and unkempt. Abby ignored the sullenness of her *onkel's* face as she threw herself into his waiting arms.

"I've missed you so much, little Abbster, and so has your *aenti.*"

Seth put her down.

"How is she, *Onkel* Seth? The truth."

Seth hesitated.

"I'm no longer a young *maidel.* I'm all grown up as you can see, and I need to see *Aenti* Lillian. Where is she?"

Her *onkel* looked worn out and defeated, but he pointed toward the back of the *haus.* "She's in bed. She won't leave the room, and cradles the *boppli's* blanket like he is still alive."

Seth choked back tears.

Lizzie stood at her *dochder's* side. "Maybe you should leave her alone. She needs time to heal."

"Please, *Onkel* Seth. I feel terrible enough for not being here when it happened." Abby lowered her voice almost to a whisper. "But I would never be able to live with myself if I didn't at least *try* to reach out to her."

Seth nodded his consent, and Abby didn't give him a chance to change his mind. She practically ran to the room where her *aenti* had holed up in since her *boppli's* unexpected death.

Abby knocked lightly on the door, but she didn't get an answer. Opening the door cautiously, she searched the darkened room for signs of her *aenti*. A noise from the corner of the room brought Abby's eyes into focus on her *aenti,* who rocked in a chair mindlessly, a blank expression spread across her face. Abby walked softly toward her, careful not to startle the woman. She placed her hand carefully across her *aenti's* arm, speaking her name quietly.

Lillian looked up at her with swollen, red-rimmed eyes. Abby knelt down beside her *aenti* just in time to embrace her as she collapsed in her arms. Abby rocked the crying woman as she hummed softly the same German lullaby her *mamm* had hummed to her well into her teens. It was the only thing Abby's *mamm* had remembered from her own *mamm* before she'd passed, and it was the only thing Abby knew to do to comfort her *aenti.*

Abby eyed the empty cradle in the opposite corner of the room, and wondered why her *onkel* had not removed such a grave reminder of their loss and packed it out of sight. She would have to broach the subject lightly to avoid upsetting him more than he already was. It broke Abby's heart that her *aenti* and *onkel* had lost their only child. Knowing they could never have any of their own had to be even more devastating. It was something Abby could only imagine, but from Lillian's sobbing, she was beginning to feel the strain of it right along with her.

After a while, Lillian's sobs turned to sniffles, and then began to subside altogether. "Every time I feel like I can't cry anymore, it seems I have more to get out. I'm sorry for losing control like that."

Abby felt badly for her. "Don't apologize, *Aenti.* Crying is *Gott's* gift to us. It allows us to release our sorrows to Him."

Lillian looked at her niece seriously. *"Gott* didn't save my *boppli.* Why?"

"None of us knows what *Gotte's Wille* is for our lives. But if we seek Him in our time of need, He will reveal His plan to us. Have you prayed about this yet, *Aenti?"*

Lillian pushed herself back into the rocking chair and held the small quilt to her face. "What's the point? My *boppli* is gone, and I can't have any more because of the surgery."

Abby moved in closer to her *aenti.* "Have you considered adopting a *boppli?* The woman who owns the bakery I worked for in Ohio has a teenage *dochder* who is pregnant. She is looking for a *familye* to adopt her *boppli.*"

At Abby's suggestion, Lillian's expression changed. "That won't bring back my *boppli.* I'm tired. Can you please go now? I need to lie down."

Abby stood, feeling worse than when she'd first seen her *aenti.* "I'm sorry if I upset you. But please think about what I said."

Lillian shooed her with her hand as she shuffled toward the bed and collapsed onto it. "Please close the door when you leave. And don't let anyone else in here. I'm too tired to visit."

Abby swallowed the lump in her throat and left the room, feeling as though she'd done more than damage to her poor *aenti* instead of helping as she'd intended to do.

Chapter 9

"What did you say to her to upset her so much, Abby?"

Abby sighed helplessly. "I might have suggested she consider adopting a *boppli.* I told her about my old boss's *dochder* who is pregnant and looking for a *familye* to adopt her *boppli.* After I said it, she asked me to leave. I'm really sorry, *Onkel* Seth. I didn't mean to make things worse."

Abby was practically in tears, but her *onkel* didn't look displeased with her admission.

"Is there any way you could arrange for us to meet this young *maidel?"*

Abby was confused. "But *Aenti* just told me she wanted me to leave her alone. I don't think she will accept a *boppli* that isn't her own."

Seth fought back tears. "She's so hurt right now; she doesn't know what she wants. But there isn't any harm in meeting with the pregnant teenager. Will you see if you can arrange it?"

Her *onkel's* enthusiasm gave Abby hope. "Of course. I'll call her just before I open the bakery in the morning. Are you sure this won't upset *Aenti* Lillian?"

"I can't be certain of anything anymore. But it doesn't hurt to explore another chance to have a *familye* with your *aenti* Lillian."

Abby hoped she hadn't started something that would cause her *aenti* more pain. The last thing she wanted to do was pour salt on the poor woman's wounds.

Abby scraped the last bit of pink frosting from the bottom of the mixing bowl and smeared it across the heart-shaped sugar cookie. She put it with the others so the frosting could set before she boxed them for potential orders throughout the day. Melanie, her old boss, at the Brick Oven Bakery in Ohio had shown her how to make the cinnamon-candy cookies for Valentine's Day the previous year. The cookies were a big item with the *Englischers,* and Abby hoped it might help bring in some new business to Lillian's small bakery.

The jingling of the bells on the front door alerted her to an early customer, but she hadn't yet turned the sign over to reveal she was open for business yet. Abby wondered who might be venturing out at such an hour. Poking her head around the corner of the kitchen, Abby spotted Becca, Jonah's sister, and her childhood friend.

A very pregnant Becca greeted her with a welcoming smile. "*Gudemariye,* cousin. My *bruder* told me I could find you here. I've missed you."

Abby pasted on a smile for her friend, even though to hear Becca call her "cousin" was irritating enough to prickle her nerves. But it wasn't like she could tell even her best friend the secret that put an end to their friendship when she left. "I missed you too, but I was afraid you wouldn't want to see me after hearing the rumors about your *bruder* and me."

Becca waved a casual hand at Abby. "That was a long time ago. But I always knew you were a different sort from the first time I met you. It didn't surprise me when I learned what happened between the two of you. I could see the way the two of you looked at each other. But I hope now that you're older and wiser that all that foolishness is behind you. After all, you left my *bruder* to confess to the Bishop alone. He took full responsibility for what happened. The Bishop told him he should have known better since he was older, but I'm just not sure my *bruder* saw it that way."

Abby couldn't deny the truth about the kiss to Becca. Her friend knew her better than that. But she had no idea what Jonah had gone through when she left. It had never dawned on her that he would have to face a confession alone. She felt terrible about it, but there was nothing to be done about it now except apologize to him.

"I never meant to cause more trouble when I left, but at the time, I thought running from my problems was my only solution. I'm sorry I hurt you in the process."

Becca picked up one of the cookies and bit into it.

"This is *wunderbaar,* cousin. I must have a box of these."

Abby cringed at the word "cousin" again. Would she ever be able to get past this? Or was she doomed to be forced to live with her *mamm's* lies for the rest of her life?

"When is the *boppli* to arrive? Is it your first?"

Becca rolled a hand over her swelling abdomen lovingly. "*Jah,* it's my first *boppli.* And he or she is due any day."

Abby felt a twinge of concern. "Should you be out on such a day if you're that close to the end of your confinement?"

Becca hugged Abby. "You will see some day when you have your own *boppli,* and you will want the distraction of visiting to keep you busy while you wait. The last few days have been the hardest for me to sit still knowing I am to be a *mamm* soon."

Abby didn't think she would ever be so lucky as to have her own *boppli* since the *mann* she loved could never be her husband. She found envy creeping into her mind, and she pushed it back and smiled for the sake of her friend.

After boxing up a fresh batch of cookies for Becca, she bid her *gut daag,* and happily sent her on her way. It wasn't that she didn't want to visit with her friend; she guessed that she needed to ease herself into her past relationships, or her nerves would not be able to withstand the added pressures she was already under with her *familye.* One *gut* thing that would come from helping her *aenti* would be that she would have less time to think about Jonah.

Jonah practically had to sit on his hands the entire day to keep from walking down to the bakery. The heavenly smells drifting on the gentle breeze was not enough to satisfy him. Not to mention his craving for looking into Abby's warm hazel eyes. Feelings of guilt soon replaced the warm thoughts of Abby, and he found himself reaching out to *Gott* like never before.

If it's a sin to love Abby, Gott, then why won't you take away these strong feelings I have for her? I surrender my wille to You, dear Gott.

Despite his prayers, the urgency to see Abby still remained deep-seated in his heart. Deciding to take a walk in the early evening air to clear his mind, he pulled his coat from the peg near the door of the barn and shoved his hat on his head before walking out into the snow.

Light snow swirled around like mosquitoes in July, the sun dipping toward the horizon. Jonah searched his mind for any scenario where he and Abby could have a normal life together as his feet crunched in the snow, but a solution eluded him. He walked with no real direction in mind, but before he realized, he faced the set of mulberry trees near the school yard. Pacing between them was Abby, who seemed to be talking to herself. Unsure of whether he should approach her, he stood back and watched her verbal struggle, wishing he could hear what she was saying.

Chapter 10

Abby paced back and forth between the mulberry trees—the very spot where she and Jonah had shared their one and only special kiss. She called out to *Gott,* begging him for a way out of this mess. For a way that she and Jonah could share more than stolen glances and forbidden kisses. With her *mamm's* lie hanging over their heads, they would never be permitted to marry, and she would never live in sin with him just for a chance to be with him. But how could she tell Jonah the truth without soiling her *mamm's* honor and reputation with the community. Not to mention what the exposed lie would do to her *daed.*

Gott, please send me a sign that you will make this right for us. I surrender my wille to You.

Abby looked up at the increasing flurries that swirled about her. Snowflakes caught on her cheeks and melted, leaving a light mist behind. As she turned toward the school house, she noticed Jonah leaning up against the building watching her. She stopped in her tracks, and waited as he slowly made his way over to her.

Jonah looked into her eyes, thinking how beautiful she looked with the snow fluttering around her and moving wisps of her auburn hair loose from her *kapp*. "What are you doing out here so late? You look cold."

Abby tipped her chin toward him, admiring his slight smile. "I should ask you the same thing."

Jonah shuffled his feet in the snow, wishing his toes would warm up. "I needed to take a walk. Clear my head of a few things."

"Becca came into the bakery this morning. She didn't stay long. But I had a lot of work to get done to prepare for my first day back. I was grateful to have a steady stream of customers today."

Jonah nodded politely. He didn't want to talk about the bakery. He wanted to know why she left. He wanted answers to questions he'd been asking himself repeatedly for the past five years. He'd missed her.

Abby pulled her knitted scarf around her head and neck to shield it from the increasing snow. "Your *schweschder* told me you had to confess to the Bishop after I left the community. I'm sorry I left you to endure that alone. I never meant to hurt you Jonah, but you shouldn't have publically exposed our sin the way you did."

Jonah kicked at the snow. "I never meant to hurt you either Abby, but I couldn't deny my love for you any longer. I acted like a foolish *kin.* I'm not even sure we should be alone now."

Jonah closed the distance between them, and Abby stood her ground. "I've missed you Abby. So much it hurts."

Abby closed her eyes as he brushed his warm cheek against hers. She wanted him to kiss her again. To kiss her like he didn't care about the consequences of the community—or the world, for that matter. What she couldn't understand was why he was so willing to risk everything to be near her when he didn't know they weren't cousins.

Abby took a step back. "We can't do this again, Jonah. We have to keep our relationship proper. If we don't, we risk excommunication."

Jonah moved in closer to her again. "It's been five long years, and I've prayed until there were no more words, begging *Gott* to make me stop loving you. Seeing you again has only made those feelings stronger. Wrong or not, I can't help how I feel."

"Your love is not wrong, Jonah." The words came out in a whisper.

Abby found it difficult to breathe around the lump in her throat. Swallowing down the tears, she asked *Gott* for the courage to walk away from Jonah. As hard as she tried, her feet wouldn't move. Instead, she tipped her heard toward Jonah's, allowing him to press his warm lips against hers ever so softly. Her breaths came in shallow puffs as she leaned into his kiss with the sort of passion she'd seen *Englischers* display when she lived in Ohio.

Abby could not deny her love for Jonah, but she couldn't betray her *mamm* at the same time. She was torn between the truth and a lie that had ruined her life in more ways than she cared to acknowledge.

Jonah suddenly pulled away. "I can't do this to you, Abby. I must do right by you this time."

Abby caught her breath. "But Jonah, you don't understand. There's something you don't know. It doesn't have to be like this. I can make it right. Just give me some time."

"Abby, no amount of time is going to change things. We could sneak around like we did before and hope we don't get caught, but what would that prove? We can't marry, which means I can't be with you the way I want to—the way I've longed to be with you for a very long time."

Tears fell down Abby's cold cheeks, worrying her they would freeze. "Jonah, I love you. I've always loved you, and I can't make it stop no matter how much I've begged *Gott* to take away the love I have for you. But I know a way we can be together. You have to trust me and give me some time."

"Abby you don't understand how guilty I feel for loving you—how guilty I've felt all these years. I don't understand why I love you differently than my other cousins. Maybe it's because I never even met you until I was thirteen years old. I know we didn't grow up together, and we've never had a traditional cousin-to-cousin relationship, but that's no excuse for way I've acted out my feelings for you. Or for the way I've jeopardized your standing in the community."

Tears pooled in Jonah's eyes. It broke Abby's heart to see him like this. Couldn't she just tell him the truth now and take care of it later with her parents? Or would the truth backfire on her and make things worse?

Jonah pressed a lingering kiss on her forehead. "I will always love you, but we can't be together. Deep down we both know it. If even *Gott* can't change the fact that we are cousins, then what hope is there?"

Jonah turned on his heel and walked away. Abby called after him, but he walked more swiftly and never turned around. Abby fell to her knees in the deep snow, sobbing uncontrollably.

Gott, please give me the strength to confront my mamm and daed. Bring the truth to light, and bless Jonah and me with a love that honors You.

Chapter 11

Abby had to stay focused on her *onkel* Seth and *aenti* Lillian, and that meant putting her own problems aside for the day. She would deal with her *mamm* later. But for now, she had to help *Aenti* Bess ready the rooms at the B&B for the arrival of Melanie and her *dochder,* Ellie tomorrow. Abby was already exhausted from a full day at the bakery, but she had promised her *familye* that she would help make this visit go as smoothly as possible.

She feared her *onkel* had gotten his hopes up about the possibility of adopting Ellie's *boppli.* And it was through no fault of her own that Abby felt responsible for the whole thing. Because of this, she'd worked hard for the past two days arranging everything from having a taxi pick Melanie and Ellie up at the train station, to arranging three rooms at the B&B for the two women and the adoption attorney—just in case.

She'd even pushed aside her own prayers to talk to *Gott* about bringing these two *mamm's* together for the sake of the *boppli's* well-being. She couldn't imagine the hurt that her *aenti* was feeling because of her loss. But if it was even a tiny bit as much as the hurt she felt for the loss of Jonah, she didn't know how her *aenti* was able to bear it.

Bess surveyed the neatness of the last room Abby cleaned. "You're a lot better at this than you were when you were a *kin*. If not for the girl I have working here, there's no way I could keep this place open. I'm thankful you were able to help me this week while she's taking her trip to see her *familye*. What do say we get some hot *kaffi* in you before you head home in the cold?"

Abby pushed stray hairs behind her ear. "That sounds *gut*. Some *kaffi* will keep me awake until my slow mare trots home."

Abby collapsed into the first chair at the small table in the kitchen. They had already cleaned the dining room for the guests, and the kitchen table was more for *familye* anyway.

Aenti Bess pushed a mug of hot *kaffi* in front of Abby, who looked like she could fall asleep in it. "What's with the long face? If this adoption is troubling you, let it go and let *Gott* have control of it. You've done all you can; the rest is up to Him."

Abby sipped her *kaffi* slowly, hoping for a little more time to think before she blurted out what was really on her mind.

Aenti Bess winked at her. "This is about a *mann,* isn't it? Perhaps a certain forbidden love that's gotten your feathers so ruffled?"

Abby swallowed hard the hot liquid, hoping it would keep her from speaking her mind.

Bess cleared her throat. "You know it wasn't that long ago that I had a similar conversation with your *mamm* at this very table. She was still so much in love with your *daed.* But she'd run off to Ohio, same as you did. While she was gone, your *daed* married her best friend. She didn't think your *daed* would ever take her back—especially since she had you. But when you ran off and went in search of Jacob, nothing else mattered to her except finding you. And when your *daed* showed up with you and everyone thought Jacob was your *daed,* he didn't deny it. He let the lie go to protect you and your *mamm.* He did the honorable thing by marrying your *mamm* that day."

Abby let a fresh tear fall unchecked. "I don't understand why he did that. And I certainly don't understand why they led me to believe he was my *daed* all those years."

Bess took her hands in hers. "They did it to protect you in case the *menner* that were after your biological father for his debt would ever come looking for you. It was to protect you."

"But I've been in Ohio for the past five years and no one came after me. Maybe there was no real danger. Or they didn't recognize me when I went there because I'd grown up. I don't know what to think. But what I do know is that lie has hurt me in a lot of ways. It's prevented me from having a life with Jonah."

Bess leaned back in her chair and crossed her arms over her ample bosom. "You have to decide if you will honor your *mamm* and *daed* as it says in the Bible, or if you will choose your own path. If you choose your own path, you will have to leave the community. And since you were just baptized a few days ago, are you prepared to leave again? Search your heart, and seek *Gott* for the answers."

Abby leaned her head down and cupped her chin with her hands. She rested her elbows on the table to support her head that threatened to slip off her tired shoulders from lack of sleep. "I've prayed so much I'm certain *Gott* is tired of hearing the same thing from me."

Bess slurped the bottom of her *kaffi*. "Then change your prayers. Whenever I don't get an answer, I change my prayers to reflect another person's needs, rather than my own. When our prayers are selfish and greedy, *Gott* has a way of making us wait for an answer until we pray for His *wille* and not our own."

Abby sat up straight. "You think I should be praying for *Mamm?* She's the cause of all this. She's the one that lied—not me. It's really hard to keep from being angry with her."

"But you were baptized. Did you confess the kiss you shared with Jonah to the Bishop before your baptism?"

Abby stood up and poured another cup of *kaffi*.

"No. I didn't feel the need to confess the kiss because it wasn't a sin. Jonah and I are *not* cousins."

Bess held her cup out to Abby for a refill. "The point is Abby, that the community views you as cousins. And unless your *mamm* and *daed* go to the Bishop and confess the lie, you will not be able to be with Jonah. So you might consider changing your prayers."

Abby finally got the point. It didn't help that she was emotionally and physically drained. But her *aenti* was painfully right about one thing—she could never ask her *mamm* to confess. She could only pray about it, and hope *Gott* would change her *mamm's* heart.

Chapter 12

Jonah paced back and forth alongside the bakery, wondering if he should go inside and talk to Abby. It had been two days since they shared the kiss under the mulberry tree, and he needed to convince her to go with him to the Bishop to confess. He'd nearly driven himself mad with worry that someone might have seen them. If that was the case, it would only be a matter of time before they were excommunicated. It was still early, and the bakery probably wouldn't be open for at least another hour, but he could smell something so *gut,* his mouth was watering. Grabbing the door handle before he lost his nerve, he swung it open, the bells jingling his presence.

Abby poked her head around the corner of the kitchen, chiding herself for forgetting to lock door behind her yet again. She wasn't ready for customers yet. When she caught sight of Jonah, her heart did a somersault.

Jonah quickly pulled his hat off his head and held it in front of him as he walked toward Abby. "I think we should talk about what happened the other night. It seems history is repeating itself, and if we don't get it under control, we'll both be excommunicated. I'm a buggy maker, and I can't make a living outside the community. *Englischers* don't have a need for buggies, and I don't know the first thing about fixing their fancy cars. My place is in the community, and I don't want to risk losing that."

Abby continued to cut heart shapes in the cookie dough and place them on the baking sheet. "I agree with you about not being able to make a living among the *Englisch,* but I won't confess to something I'm not sorry for."

Jonah grabbed one of the heart-shaped cookies with pink frosting and shoved a bite of it in his mouth to keep his hands occupied. "Don't worry, I'll pay for it," he said around the cookie in his mouth.

Abby turned to him playfully. "You better."

Her smile melted his heart. He set his hat and the cookie on the counter and pulled Abby into his arms. He kissed the top of her hair that smelled like sugar cookies, moving his lips to her forehead, and then down her cheek.

"*Gott* help me, Abby, I love you, and I don't know how to stop."

Abby didn't try to resist Jonah's advances. She wanted him to hold her and never let her go. Tilting her head until her lips met his, she tasted the sweet frosting from the cookie. The sweetness of his mouth somehow tasted better than the cookie, and she continued to kiss him with a hunger for it.

But once again, Jonah pushed her away from him.

"Abby, we can't do this every time we see each other. I've written my *onkel* in Florida about the possibility of going to live there in his community. I was undecided, but it's obvious we can't stay in this community together and keep a level of propriety in our relationship. It's probably better if I leave after I confess to the Bishop next Saturday. I guess it's better if we say our goodbyes now."

Abby fell back against the counter, feeling as though she'd had the wind knocked out of her. Tears welled up in her eyes as she looked at Jonah. The front of his coat was covered in flour from her apron, his eyes cast to the floor. She couldn't tell him the truth now; it would seem like a desperate attempt to keep him here. But she couldn't just stand by and let him leave before she had a chance to fix the situation either.

"Jonah, please don't leave. I told you I can fix this. I can't tell you how, but I'm going to very soon if you'll just trust me."

"I can't stay here near you when all I want to do is hold you and kiss you. It's not right, Abby, and I won't sneak around like a sinner waiting to get caught. You need to move on with your life. I'll always love you, but I have to go. Goodbye Abby." His voice was weak and tearful.

Before Abby could say another word, he placed a dollar on the counter, picked up his hat and walked briskly toward the door.

Abby struggled to move her feet and find her voice, but she was filled with too much trepidation to function. She tried calling after him, but it was too late.

The door closed and he was gone.

Anger filled Abby, and she grabbed several of the heart-shaped cookies in both hands and smashed them against the opposite wall. She wished she'd never come back to the community.

Lizzie followed the sound of soft crying that led to Abby's bedroom door. Lifting her hand to knock, she paused, wondering if talking to her *dochder* would do either of them any *gut*. Abby had gone straight to her room after coming home early from the bakery, and she didn't even come down for the evening meal. Lizzie knew what was troubling her *dochder,* and it was *her* fault.

Dear Gott, give me the strength to do the right thing where Abby is concerned. Bless me with the courage to do the right thing. Show me how to make things right for her and Jonah.

Chapter 13

At two o'clock, Abby turned the *Closed* sign over on the door of the bakery and locked the door. She had planned to meet Melanie for a late lunch at the B&B while her *aenti* and *onkel* met with Ellie about the adoption. It was hard to feel excited about seeing her old boss and friend, but she had to push her feelings about Jonah aside for the time-being and put her trust in *Gott* to make things right. That wasn't an easy task either, given the fact that Jonah planned to leave the community in only a few days.

As Abby stacked the last of the pans in the deep sink to soak while she tidied up the rest of the kitchen for the day, she heard the jingle of bells on the front door. She froze in place for a minute, trying to remember if she'd locked the door. She was sure she had. The only other person who had a key was Lillian.

Abby grabbed a broom from the corner and walked slowly around the corner to the dining room of the bakery.

Lillian held up her hands in mock defense. "It's just me; put the broom down!"

Abby looked at the broom, which she still held above her head like a baseball bat, and smiled as she lowered it. "Sorry. I guess I'm a little jumpy. Why aren't you at the B&B? Where's *Onkel* Seth?"

Lillian looked at her with tearful eyes. "I told him I'd meet him there. But the truth is, I'm not sure I can go."

Abby took Lillian's hands in hers. "No one is forcing you to go, *Aenti.* And just because you meet her doesn't mean you're obligated to adopt the *boppli.*"

Lillian rested her head on Abby's shoulder. "I think your *onkel* will be disappointed in me if I don't go along with this."

Abby smoothed her *aenti's* hair. "That doesn't sound like *Onkel.* I think he just wants you to be happy is all."

Lillian pulled away from Abby and wiped her eyes.

"Enough about me. Tell me what's gotten you so down."

Abby had hoped her mood had not been so obvious, but she wasn't about to unload her problems on her *aenti* when the woman was still mourning the loss of her *boppli.*

"It's nothing I can't work out easily."

Lillian raised an eyebrow. "Does this have anything to do with Jonah packing up his things and closing down his business? I heard he's leaving for Florida next week."

Abby tried to contain her emotions. "I don't want to talk about it, *Aenti.*"

"Does Jonah know you two are not cousins?"

Abby felt the shock of her *aenti's* statement like a strong, winter wind. "Jonah doesn't know, but how did *you* know we aren't cousins?"

"I've suspected for a while, Abby, but that doesn't matter. What matters is how you're going to handle the situation."

Abby threw her hands up in defeat. "There's nothing I can do. If I tell Jonah the truth, I'll be betraying my *mamm.* But if I stand by and do nothing, he's going to leave. I don't want him to leave. I love him so much it hurts."

"Does he love you?"

Abby fought back tears. "Yes. He told me he still loves me, and he's leaving because he thinks that our love is a sin."

"Abby, you can't let him think he's a sinner. You have to tell him the truth or he will never trust you. You're not being fair to him—or to yourself."

"But if I expose the truth, it won't be fair to my *mamm.* No matter what I do, someone is going to be hurt."

Lillian shook her head with disgust. "Only *Gott* can show you what is the right path to take, but I think you need to have a talk with your *mamm.* Maybe she will fix it."

Abby could see that *Aenti* Lillian focusing on *her* problems instead of her own was a good distraction for her *aenti.*

"Will you help me talk to my *mamm?"*

Lillian smiled weakly. "Of course I will. I'll do anything to help you. And if I help you, it might take my mind off my own troubles."

Abby smiled. "Funny, but I was thinking the same thing about you."

Lillian hugged her niece again. "Why don't we help each other? Maybe together we can figure everything out."

"That sounds like a *gut* idea."

Lillian moved over to the sink full of dirty cake pans and pie tins. "Why don't we start with these dishes, and then you can give me a ride over to the B&B so I can meet with Ellie."

Abby didn't waste any time at all. She picked up an extra apron and tossed it to her *aenti,* and the two of them made light work of dishes.

Everything wasn't settled yet, but Abby felt better about Jonah. Finally, she had someone on *her* side. Someone to help her figure out what would be the right thing to do. Maybe, just maybe she could keep Jonah from leaving. But was it too soon to hope that they could have a future together?

Chapter 14

Jonah rushed through his day, trying to finish the last two buggies he'd been making to fill his existing orders. He'd turned down four orders for new buggies in the past two days, and he hoped he wouldn't regret it. He knew he could use a little extra money to relocate to Florida, but if he stayed to make four more buggies, it would be Spring before he was able to leave the community. And that would mean more chances that he'd fall back into sinful desires for Abby, which would, in turn, lead to being excommunicated. Then he wouldn't have anywhere to go after his *onkel* in Florida heard of his actions. No, it was best to finish what he'd started, and leave as planned.

For the past few days, Jonah had rehearsed what he'd say to the Bishop when he went to confess. He was sure the Bishop would demand discipline, but would probably wave it in lieu of his departure from the community. Jonah wished it could be another way, but he didn't see how. But what was it Abby had said about trusting her? Did he dare hope there was a way out of having to confess to something he wasn't sorry for? And was it too much to hope that *Gott* would bring a miracle to their lives? After all the praying he'd done, he could only hope.

Kneeling down, Jonah double-checked the rear wheel to be sure it would not come loose from the axle. Distracted by his thoughts, Jonah didn't notice the buggy door slipping from the clutches of the vice above his head before it was too late. He knew better than to leave the door teetering on top of the buggy while he jostled the carriage, but it was too late to rethink his error in judgment. Pain seared through his skull as the heavy wooden frame of the door fell from the roof of the buggy and connected with his head.

Taking a deep breath, Jonah pushed to his feet, feeling a sudden need for fresh air. He staggered out of the barn and into the snow-filled yard, feeling as though his wobbly legs couldn't carry him any further. The corners of his vision began to turn dark, but as hard as he fought to keep focus, it was no use. Coldness assaulted him as the darkness engulfed him.

≫≪

Abby boxed the last of the heart-shaped, frosted sugar cookies and set them aside for Jonah. She hoped that the distraction of the cookies would give her enough time to talk him into changing his mind about leaving the community.

When she was satisfied with the cleanliness of the bakery, she turned off the lights and locked the door behind her. Pulling her scarf tightly to shield her face from the wind, Abby headed up the long drive toward Jonah's barn at the other end of the property. Knowing it would be dark soon, she hoped her visit would also gain an offer from Jonah to drive her home after they talked.

As she neared the curve of the drive, just beyond the large oak trees that stood like sentinels at either side of the footpath, she noticed Jonah exiting the barn. Happy to see him, she picked up her pace a little. She waved, but he didn't seem to notice her. His gait seemed off balance, and bright red smeared his blonde hair like paint from a barn. But how would he have gotten paint in his hair, and where had it come from?

Was it blood?

Abby dropped the box of cookies and ran the rest of the way toward Jonah, but she did not reach him in time. She watched helplessly as he collapsed face-down into the snow. Her feet struggled to gain any headway on the icy path. When she reached him, his face was half-buried in the snow, his body too calm. She dropped to her knees and began to push frantically at the snow, fearing it prevented him from breathing. A low groan escaped his blue lips. A good sign.

"Jonah, can you hear me?"

Abby jiggled him. "Jonah, please; open your eyes."

Abby pushed with all her strength to roll Jonah onto his back, hoping to get a better look at his injury. Pulling a handkerchief from the pocket of her coat, she gently mopped at the icy blood that dripped down his forehead. She looked around, knowing there was no one within shouting distance to help her, and decided she would have to drag him into the barn alone. She needed to get him out of the cold wind and warmed up so he didn't go into shock. She also knew Jonah had a phone in the barn for his business. She hoped he hadn't disconnected it in preparation for leaving.

Abby's legs felt weak, her breathing ragged from a combination of being cold and fearing for Jonah's safety. But she was determined to get him inside the shelter of the barn no matter what it took.

Gott, please give me the strength to move Jonah into the safety of the barn, and please don't let him die.

Crouching behind him, she looped her arms under his armpits, heaving him a step at a time until he lay just inside the barn. Grabbing a wool blanket that hung over the horse stall, she tucked it around Jonah, and then she wriggled out of her coat and placed it under his head. When she moved his head, he groaned again, and it was a sound Abby was happy to hear. She'd been happier if he'd opened his eyes. She prayed it would happen soon.

When Jonah was settled comfortably, Abby stood, picked up the phone, and held it to her ear, relieved to hear a dial tone. But who should she call? Every minute care was delayed; Jonah was losing blood from the deep gash in the side of his head. She dialed Dr. Davis's *haus* first, hoping he would advise her. After what seemed like an eternity on the line with the doctor's wife, she learned he was at the B&B checking on Ellie. She hung up and dialed her *aenti* Bess, happy that the doctor was there. She knew the trip to Jonah's place would only take the doctor a few minutes to reach them instead of nearly an hour form his own farm.

Tears welled up in her eyes as she waited for the doctor to come to the phone. Jonah seemed lifeless as he lay on the floor of the barn, and that frightened her.

"This is Dr. Davis."

"This is Abby Yoder. I'm at Jonah Beiler's *haus*. He passed out and he has a deep cut on his head. It's bleeding a lot. I don't know what to do."

"Is he awake?"

"No! He's breathing, but the cut won't stop bleeding."

"I need you to apply pressure to the wound, and try to wake him up. I'll be there in just a few minutes."

"Please hurry!"

Abby hung up the phone and rushed to Jonah's side, praying the doctor would make it in time to mend him.

Chapter 15

Jonah moved in and out of consciousness, trying desperately to cling to Abby's angelic voice. She was praying in between crying and whispering declarations of love in his ear. Did he know why she was crying? Was he dreaming? He wished he could open his eyes and comfort her, but the pain in his head kept him from reaching out. The pressure in his head caused him to groan.

"Stay with me, Jonah. Please don't leave me. I love you."

Her voice was like butterflies fluttering above his head, but he was too cold for that to be the case. Maybe it was more like snowflakes. Jonah shivered and groaned from the pain.

"Jonah please wake up. I need you to know how much I love you."

Jonah tried to open his mouth to say it back to her, but he just couldn't form the words. He felt her love in the warm clutches of her hand on his. Was she really next to him, holding his hand? He could feel her warm breath in his ear, and smelled the baking spices he always enjoyed whenever she was near. A muffled noise that sounded like the door to his barn opening startled him out of his reverie. Then there was another voice—a male. The voice was familiar, but he struggled to place it. Abby was telling the man he'd gotten hurt. It was Doctor Davis.

Jonah suddenly remembered the buggy door falling on his head. The last thing he remembered was trying to get a little fresh air. Was he bleeding? A vague memory plagued him of feeling blood dripping down his face before seeing it land in the snow at his feet—just before he fell. And now he could hear Doctor Davis asking Abby to help him clean his head wound. Is that why his head hurt so much? Had the door cut open his head when it landed on him?

Abby watched Doctor Davis sponge a cleansing solution over the wound on Jonah's head while she tried not to become squeamish. "Is he going to need stitches?"

"I'm afraid so. He'll also need to be monitored for the next twenty-four hours. If he doesn't wake up, he could slip into a coma. The fact that he's groaning means that he can feel some of the pain, and hopefully that's enough to keep him out of danger. I'll let him sleep until I'm done stitching him up since I don't have any Novocain to numb him."

Abby gasped. "Does that mean he's going to feel it when you stitch him up?"

"It's possible, but he probably won't remember it when he wakes up."

Abby hated the thought of Jonah being able to feel the doctor stitching up his wound, but she knew it couldn't be avoided. If he didn't get the bleeding under control soon, it could put him at further risk.

When the doctor tied the last stitch, he reached into his bag and retrieved smelling salts. "You might want to take a step back. I've seen patients flail around when this stuff is placed under their nose."

Abby did as she was instructed, hoping it would work to wake Jonah without startling him.

Please, Gott, let him wake up.

It took a minute, but Jonah soon stirred. He groaned as his eyelids fluttered. His hand reached toward the wound on his head, but the doctor stopped him from touching the stitches.

"Hold on Jonah, I need to bandage your head to keep infection out. Lie still for just another minute."

The sound of Jonah's phone ringing startled Abby. She looked to him. "Should I answer that?"

Doctor Davis nodded and chuckled. "It could be someone looking for me since my services seem to be much needed today."

Abby answered it. "This is Abby Yoder."

"This is Levi Graber. Your *aenti* at the B&B told me Doctor Davis went over there because Jonah is injured. Is everything alright?"

Abby wasn't sure how much she should tell Levi, fearing it might worry Becca unnecessarily. "He got a few stitches in his head, but he's talking to the doctor now. How is Becca?"

"That's the reason I'm calling. Becca is in labor. We need the doctor over here as soon as possible."

"Hold on a minute." Abby put her hand over the receiver and told Doctor Davis what was going on.

Jonah struggled. "I need to get up. I have to go to my *schweschder*."

Doctor Davis put a firm hand on Jonah's shoulder.

"You won't be going anywhere for a few days, so be still while I bandage you up." He looked to Abby. "Ask Levi how far apart the contractions are."

After talking with Levi another minute, Abby put her hand back over the receiver of the phone. "He said about thirty minutes apart."

"Tell Levi I'll be there in about an hour. It sounds like she has a while to go yet."

Abby relayed the doctor's message to Levi, and told him to send her love to Becca, and for her not to worry because her *bruder* was in *gut* hands.

Jonah groaned again. "How bad is it, Doc?"

The doctor looked at him over the glasses that rested low on his nose. "Thirty-seven stitches. And on top of that, you have a concussion. You'll be off your feet for at least three days. That is if we can keep this cut from getting infected."

Jonah tried to smile, but winced from the pain.

"Thirty-seven, huh? That's ten more than my knee when I was twelve, remember?"

Doctor Davis chuckled. "I see your memory is intact. That's a good sign. But you'll still have to be watched. I imagine since your sister seems to be in labor, and you don't have any other family here, you could probably talk your cousin here into staying with you for a couple of days. She's the one that found you. She's an excellent nurse-maid. You're lucky she found you as quickly as she did, or things might have been worse."

Abby blushed at the thought of staying with Jonah. She knew her parents would never allow her to stay with Jonah without a chaperone, but she couldn't let him down. Caleb would not be able to take time from work to stay with him, and that left only her. She knew it would mean closing the bakery for a few days, but maybe this was all part of *Gott's* plan. She hoped Lillian would agree to go back to the bakery in her absence, knowing her *aenti* would heal faster with the bakery to tend to. And Jonah would heal faster with Abby to tend to his care. After all, the doctor himself had suggested it, but perhaps if Rachel came along, her parents would permit it.

Chapter 16

"I'm a grown woman, and capable of making my own choices, *Mamm.* I'm going to stay with Jonah while he heals, and I'll bring Rachel with me as a chaperone. You might be able to get in the way of my marrying Jonah, but I cannot let you prevent me from making certain he survives this crisis."

Her *mamm* sank onto the bed while Abby packed a few of her belongings. "I didn't know you wanted to marry him, Abby. Why didn't you tell me things were so serious between the two of you?"

Abby pursed her lips. She did not want to have this conversation now. She needed to hurry back to Jonah and relieve Doctor Davis so he could get over to Becca's *haus* to deliver her *boppli.*

"It doesn't matter because we can never be together since the community thinks we're cousins. Do you have any idea how guilty Jonah feels for loving me the way he does? He thinks he's a sinner! And I can't do anything to make him stop from feeling that way unless I betray your honor."

Abby began to cry. "I will never love another *mann* the way I love Jonah, so I am destined to become a spinster. So I will be a burden on *Daed* for the rest of my life—or the rest of his, whichever ends first. But I'm certain it will be me because I will probably die from a broken heart before old age can claim me."

Lizzie tried to comfort her *dochder,* but there were no words that would undo the damage her lies had caused. How had she missed the new developments in their relationship since Abby had returned? What could she do to make up for the damage? Could she possibly go to the Bishop and confess? Was it too late to salvage things for Abby and Jonah?

"I'm sorry, Abby. I never meant for you to be hurt in any of this."

"Well I am hurt, *Mamm.* And Jonah and I continue to be hurt. The only thing that will fix this is having the truth out in the open to the Bishop and the entire community."

There. She'd said it. She wasn't proud of her disrespectful suggestion, but she couldn't hold it in any longer.

Lizzie hung her head. "I'm not sure I can do that, Abby. It might make things worse—especially for your *daed.*"

Abby gathered her things in her arms and placed them in her childhood suitcase. "He isn't my *daed.* My *father* is a dead drug-dealer. Say it *mother.* I want to hear you say it out loud to me. You couldn't even say it five years ago when I found out the truth. I'm still surprised you admitted it to me at all. Why did you? It would have been better if I'd never known. At least that way I would know there was nothing keeping me from marrying Jonah."

"I'm sorry, Abby."

"Sorry doesn't fix this mess. Sorry doesn't allow me and Jonah to marry. Sorry won't mend my broken heart."

Abby picked up her things and went to the door.

"Are you going to let Rachel go with me?"

Lizzie nodded her consent, tears filling her eyes when Abby walked away without saying another word.

Abby left word with *Aenti* Bess to have her *aenti* Lillian stop by Jonah's *haus* after she and *Onkel* Seth left the B&B so she could let her know she wouldn't be able to work at the bakery for a few days. She hated to let Lillian down after she'd promised to work for her, but it had already been closed more than a month before she'd returned from Ohio.

After settling herself and Rachel into the room Jonah assigned to them, the two of them busied themselves in the kitchen preparing a light meal for Jonah. The doctor had suggested a diet consisting of mostly liquids until tomorrow. Abby found ingredients to make chicken soup and biscuits with honey. Feeling comfortable in Jonah's modest *haus,* Abby wondered what it would be like if she was able to live there with him as his *fraa.*

Please Gott, make a way for Jonah and me to be married. I want to be his fraa more than anything.

Abby carried a tray to Jonah's room and knocked lightly on the door. It hadn't been easy helping the doctor get Jonah up the stairs, especially since he had to stop frequently to quell dizziness and nausea. But Jonah had stubbornly insisted he be able to convalesce in his own bed. She didn't blame him. He would never have been comfortable on the sofa downstairs, and he would probably not be a cooperative patient without proper rest.

At Jonah's groan, Abby entered the room cautiously. Setting the tray at the end of the bed, she blushed at the sight of him lying helplessly in the bed built for two. The doctor had removed Jonah's blood-stained shirt, and he lay there with his torso exposed. Abby admired his muscular build, noting that he was no longer the young boy she'd fallen in love with as a teenager. Thankful his eyes were closed so he couldn't see the deep blush that painted her cheeks with fire, she continued to admire him until he cleared his throat. The noise startled her, bringing more heat to her already pink cheeks.

Abby straightened, rethinking her decision to stay with Jonah. If not for her *mamm's* lies, she would already be his *fraa,* and she would be able to lie next to him and cradle him in her arms. She had to keep a clear head or she was going to fall into temptation, and she didn't want that any more than Jonah would.

Seeing that his eyes were now wide open, she motioned to the tray at the foot of the bed. "Can you sit up for a few minutes and eat a little something? I made you some chicken soup and biscuits."

Jonah tried to smile, but couldn't manage it with the amount of pain he was in. "Smells *gut.* I can try. Can you push the extra pillow behind me?"

Abby reached for the pillow, wishing she'd walked over to the opposite side of the bed to get it. With her hand on the pillow, her face was close to Jonah's—too close. He looked at her with hopeful eyes, and she knew he wanted to kiss her just as much as she wanted to be kissed. He reached for her, but the pain in his head won. He winced, and Abby picked up the pillow and readied it behind him while he attempted to straighten himself in the bed.

"I hate that you went to all this trouble for me. I'm not sure I can stomach anything beyond the broth in the soup."

Abby smiled. "Not to worry. Rachel is downstairs eating your portion, and will probably devour my portion as well if I don't return soon."

Abby held the bowl up for him while he painstakingly took hold of the spoon and attempted to bring it to his mouth. "I don't know why I feel so weak. Maybe it's because this headache hasn't subsided. The doc gave me something for it, but it hasn't helped yet."

Abby smiled. "The doctor said you would feel weak and groggy for a few days. You lost quite a lot of blood and you have a concussion. I can help you; that's what I'm here for."

Abby lifted a spoonful of broth to his full lips, wishing she could kiss them just one last time.

Who was she trying to fool?

There was no way she could live without this *mann*, and she had a plan to make sure she wouldn't have to. When he was well, she intended to tell him the truth about everything—no matter the consequences.

Chapter 17

Abby pushed the button on her wind-up alarm beside the large bed she shared with Rachel, and pushed herself from the warmth of the quilt. Holding up the face of the clock toward the moonlight, she noted the time, and reset the alarm for six o'clock. She'd been in to wake Jonah every two hours as the doctor ordered to be sure he didn't slip into a coma, and to check the dressing for signs of bleeding.

Exhausted, she forced her feet down the hall to Jonah's room. She hated to wake him again, but no matter how cruel it seemed, it was necessary. Each time, she'd knock lightly, get no answer, and then enter his room anyway. The first time, she'd felt shy, but now that it was four o'clock in the morning, she was ready to get it over with and get a little more sleep before having to start her busy day.

Abby crept into the room, letting the moonlight guide her to Jonah's side. The quilt had slipped to his waist, and she watched the gentle rise and fall of his diaphragm for a minute, admiring his well-formed abdominal muscles. As she reached for the edge of the quilt to cover him, her hand grazed his heated skin. He was too warm. Placing the back of her hand under his chin and across his forehead, she realized he was burning up with fever.

Abby snatched the battery-operated thermometer from the bedside table that Doctor Davis had left for her, and tucked it under his arm. She held it there for several minutes. Jonah groaned and tried to wriggle free from the light pressure she placed on his shoulder to hold the thermometer in place.

"Jonah, can you wake up? I need you to open your eyes for me for just a minute if you can."

Jonah moved and groaned. "I'm cold."

Abby pulled the thermometer from his armpit and shined the doctor's flashlight on it to read it. Abby became alarmed when she saw it was 102.8 degrees.

"Jonah, you have a fever." Her voice seemed suddenly loud in the quietness of the night.

"I'm cold," Jonah mumbled again.

Abby pulled up the quilt and tucked it under his chin, but she needed to do something to bring his fever down. Then she remembered her *daed* packing snow around her when she had a bad case of the flu that first winter she'd come to live in the community.

Abby placed a hand on Jonah's shoulder and let him know she'd be back in a minute.

He didn't respond.

Racing down the stairs to the kitchen, Abby searched the cupboards for something large enough to put snow into. Finding a large canning pot that had most likely belonged to his *mamm,* Abby held it close to her as she pushed her feet into her boots that she'd left by the back door, and then slipped her arms into her coat.

The moon shone bright against the white snow, illuminating the quiet yard. Packing as much snow as she could into the oversized pot, she lifted it, surprised at how heavy it was. Realizing it was going to take several trips to get as much snow as she needed to pack around Jonah to cool him, she considered waking Rachel to help, but figured it would probably take more time than doing the job herself.

By the time Abby reached Jonah's room with the fifth pot of snow, she was so out of breath, she feared she would not be able to continue, but she was determined get as much as possible. But even after she finished, she would have to mop up the trail of slush she'd left from the back door to Jonah's room by leaving her boots on during each trip. She could have removed them, but time was crucial, and she didn't mind mopping up the mess later. She was, however, grateful Jonah's floors were all wood and linoleum between the back door and Jonah's room.

Packing the last bit of snow over the section of quilt that was tucked closely around his neck, she noted that some of the snow had already melted and was soaking through the quilt. She felt bad for Jonah as she watched him shiver, his teeth chattering almost non-stop.

Abby feared for Jonah more, as it was obvious infection had set in the wound as the doctor had warned. She kissed his warm forehead, tears pooling in her eyes.

Please Gott, save Jonah's life, and spare him from any more pain.

Chapter 18

Promptly at seven o'clock, Doctor Davis arrived as promised. It had been a long night for Abby, and she'd just poured a third cup of *kaffi* when the aging doctor tapped lightly on the back door.

Abby opened the door.

"How's the patient this morning?"

"I've had him packed in snow for the last few hours, and the fever is starting to come down."

Abby had finally had to wake Rachel to help her, as the snow was melting almost as quickly as she could get it to him. With the two of them working, they'd been able to keep a constant packing of fresh snow for the past few hours. The continuous running up and down the stairs had all but worn Abby out.

Rachel was back in bed, and she didn't have the heart to disturb her. Abby figured with the doctor there, she might as well let Rachel sleep for an hour.

"I brought some medicine to bring down the fever, and I'll have to ride into town and pick up some antibiotics for him." He followed Abby to Jonah's room.

"How's Becca? The *boppli?*"

"A healthy *buwe.* Named him Adam. Becca is worn out, but in *gut* health. She was anxious to be here with her *bruder,* but I told her not to worry, that he was in *gut* care with his cousins. She seemed a little concerned about that, but I told her not to worry because you're very capable of taking care of him."

Abby knew why Becca was concerned about her staying with her *bruder* after the conversation they'd had the day before at the bakery. But she couldn't worry about that now. She'd made sure she brought Rachel with her to establish a sense of propriety, even if it may appear not to be enough. Her only concern for the time being was nursing Jonah back to health.

Under the wet quilt, Jonah shivered and groaned.

"Can you get him up and help him change into some dry clothes? I need to put dry linens on the bed."

Abby left the room to get dry bedding, which she'd noticed in the bureau of the room she shared with her *schweschder.* When she returned, she knocked to see if the doctor was finished helping

Jonah change. When she entered, Doctor Davis was helping Jonah get into a fresh night shirt. Abby averted her eyes, fearing she would blush at the sight of his bare chest. She went straight to the bed and began to change the linens. She hurried when she heard Jonah groaning from the pain.

"I need to get back to bed; I feel pretty dizzy. Is that normal, Doc?"

Doctor Davis tucked himself under Jonah's arm and walked him back to his freshly made bed. "It might take about a week for the dizziness to go away. I'll give you some more pain medication, and hopefully that will help you sleep. Rest is what you need now to recover. I'm going to pick up some antibiotics this morning, and I will be back as soon as I can. In the meantime, it looks like your nurse here is doing a fine job of putting you on the road to recovery."

Jonah managed a weak smile for Abby, and her heart did a somersault behind her ribcage. Almost immediately, Jonah fell back asleep, so Abby walked Doctor Davis out of the room and paused for a minute in the kitchen.

"Is he out of the woods yet? Or is he still at risk because of the infection?"

Concern furrowed the doctor's brow. "I'm not going to lie to you, Abby; he still has a long recovery ahead of him. It might take days for the antibiotics to make him well enough to get out of bed for longer than a few minutes. He's lucky to have such a caring *cousin.*"

Abby's pulse raced. There was something in the way Doctor Davis said that word that alerted her. "You *know* that Jonah and I aren't cousins?"

The man flashed a hesitant look. "Your folks told me several years ago when you had a really bad case of the flu. They thought it might be important for me to put it in the medical records in case it was ever needed. I wasn't sure if you knew, or I wouldn't have suggested you stay here with Jonah."

Abby was a little upset. "How many other people in the community know?"

"As far as I know, I'm the only one. I don't believe the Bishop knows. And judging by the way Jonah acts around you, I'm guessing he doesn't know either. I can tell he loves you, but he carries a sorrowful look that reveals his broken heart. I know the two of you have a history; I'm glad you have Rachel here with you."

"I plan on telling Jonah the truth as soon as he's well enough to handle it. I can't let him leave the community because he can't bear to be around me."

The doctor placed a hand on Abby's shoulder. "Do you think that's wise to expose your folk's confidence like that? That also might have a negative impact on the way the community views you for staying here with him. Just because my wife and I are *Englisch,* doesn't mean I don't adhere to the rules of the community, and I'm certain they would frown upon such a thing. "

Abby's eyes began to tear up and her throat constricted. ""I'm not too concerned what the community thinks of me at the moment. All I care about is helping Jonah get back on his feet. I love him and I want to marry him, but I can't do that if the Bishop believes us to be first cousins. This secret has gone on long enough. I no longer need protection from my *real* father since he's been dead for fifteen years. The truth will save Jonah and me a lot of hurt."

The doctor pulled on his heavy coat. "There doesn't seem to be an easy way out of this situation. Even if the truth comes out, people in the community might be reluctant to see you and Jonah as anything other than cousins. I know you didn't come to the community until you were older, but that doesn't mean they aren't used to the idea of you being cousins. It might take folks a lot longer to come around to the truth if it should be known to them."

"I know there will be consequences no matter what happens, but I can't keep letting Jonah think his love for me is a sin. That's why he's planning on leaving,"

"I don't think he should think about traveling for at least two weeks. I'd like him to stick around until his stitches are ready to come out, but that will be up to him."

Abby was relieved to hear that she had a little extra time to sort things out, even though she felt bad that Jonah's accident was the reason.

Chapter 19

Abby placed a cool rag on Jonah's forehead, allowing her hands to linger on his warm skin. He was still fighting the fever and was due for another dose of medicine, but she hated to keep disturbing him. He'd only gone to sleep about an hour before, after a fitful afternoon of trying to withstand the pain of his headache. The pain meds were barely taking the edge off, but Jonah had refused anything stronger, claiming he preferred to stay as alert as possible. She didn't blame him for that, except she suspected it was so he could take advantage of the little bit of time they had left together before he left the community.

Abby planned on telling him the truth at some point in the next two days, since he wouldn't need her to stay with him any longer than that. Rachel had originally viewed their stay as a vacation from her regular chores at home, but she'd soon found out she'd traded one set of chores for another. And with Abby relying on her so heavily, Rachel had voiced her resistance on more than one occasion already.

Jonah stirred, the corners of his mouth struggling to form a weak smile. Abby appreciated the effort, smiling back fully. "You feel up to swallowing a few pills? It's time for your medicine. Doctor Davis was here while you were sleeping and brought the antibiotics. And since you feel warm again, you need to take another dose of the Tylenol to bring your fever down."

Jonah tried to sit up a little, but struggled against the pain. "I can't believe how much my head hurts. Maybe I need some fresh air."

"I'm not sure it's wise to go outside, but I can open the window if you think you can handle the cold. It's snowing again."

"*Denki.* I'd like it if you'd open the window. You can always get me an extra quilt if I get too cold."

Abby smiled. She was enjoying taking care of Jonah, and it made her happy that he was depending on her. She couldn't help but wish things could be different for the two of them. That they could have a normal relationship—one that wouldn't bring shame to her *mamm* and *daed.*

Abby poured the pills into Jonah's hand, and then gave him a glass of water. It saddened her to see the strain it caused him to swallow three little pills, but she prayed they would be swift to bring healing to his body. When he handed her back the glass, she placed it on the bedside table, and then started to leave his side, but he set his hand on hers.

"Wait. Don't go."

Abby smiled at his neediness. "I'm just going over to open the window for you."

His hand lingered on hers. "Make sure you come back over here when you're done. I want to talk to you."

Abby shook her head firmly. "There will plenty of time to talk in a few days once you begin to recover. You need your rest—doctor's orders."

"The doc isn't here. And maybe this can't wait."

Abby placed her hands on her hips. "Just because Doctor Davis isn't here to tell you what to do doesn't mean I'm going to let you go against his orders. This accident has caused me to do a lot of thinking. I've never been so afraid as I was when I thought I could lose you. So I'm going to make certain that you follow the doctor's orders."

"By the way, how's my *schweschder?*"

Abby turned around and smiled. "She had a healthy *buwe*. His name is Adam."

"That was my *daed's* name. He would have been so happy to have *grandkinner* named after him. I miss him and my *mamm* so much."

"I don't imagine it's easy to have both your parents gone. Your *daed* was a *gut* man. I'm sure he's looking down from heaven with a smile for little Adam."

Jonah held a weak hand out to her. After opening the window, she moved to the side of the bed and put her hand in his. He pulled gently on her hand until she sat on the edge of the bed next to him. Her cheeks heated as her thigh brushed against his even though a thick quilt separated them.

"Abby, I want to apologize for putting your honor in jeopardy. The other day when I saw you by the mulberry tree—our tree, all those feelings from the past came rushing back to me."

Abby interrupted him. "Jonah, I don't think we should be discussing this right now. You might not know what you're saying because of the fever."

Jonah pushed her hand to his forehead. "I think my fever broke about ten minutes ago. I'm fine. I'm not going to break if you talk to me. I really need to get this out in the open."

Abby pulled her hand back from his face, which was cool to the touch. "You have five minutes to say what you have to, and then you're going to rest."

Jonah tried to smile, and Abby could tell he was already worn out, but she would indulge him for a few minutes.

"What I was trying to say is that I'm sorry for treating you disrespectfully. I should never have put either of us in that situation."

Abby put her hand on his. "You weren't disrespectful. I encouraged the attention because I love you."

"I love you too, Abby, but we both need to face the truth."

Abby jumped from the edge of the bed. "The truth is…" She stood by the window, unable to finish her sentence.

Jonah patted the edge of the bed. "*Kume,* sit back down and talk to me about this without getting upset."

Reluctantly turning around to face him, Abby swallowed the tears that threatened to spill. Jonah patted the bed again, motioning her with his eyes to sit.

Jonah looked at her sorrowfully. "I don't want to hurt you anymore than I already have. I should have never let our relationship get this far out of hand. All it's done is hurt both of us. I don't want you to be hurt anymore. The sooner we face the truth, the better it will be for both of us. And the truth is, we can never marry because we're cousins."

Abby placed another hand on Jonah's head to be sure his fever had truly broken. She didn't want him to misunderstand what she was about to say.

"The truth is that we are *not* cousins at all."

Jonah turned pale. "Abby that's not funny. You shouldn't joke about that. How do you figure we aren't cousins?"

Abby took a deep breath and held it for a minute. When she let it out with a whoosh, all her anxiety went with it. "We aren't cousins because Jacob Yoder is not my real *daed*. My real *daed* is an *Englischer* named Eddie Monroe."

Jonah sat up suddenly, ignoring the intense pain in his head. "What are you saying? That you've known all this time we weren't cousins, and you let me suffer through the agony of wanting you and thinking I could never have you?"

"I left the community when I found out five years ago. When I came home, I thought it was over between us, so I didn't say anything. But when I talked to you the other day, I realized we both still had strong feelings for each other, and I prayed about it for the right way to handle the situation. I didn't mean for you to be hurt by any of this, but I didn't want to tell you that the reason we couldn't be together was because of a lie my own *mamm* had told. I felt like I was betraying both of you."

Jonah held her hand tightly. "Go with me to Florida. We can be together there."

Abby couldn't answer him. She'd run away once already and that didn't solve the problem. But she had to admit, the chance to marry Jonah held more weight with her emotions at the moment.

The sound of breaking dishes from outside the bedroom door caused Abby to jump from the edge of Jonah's bed.

Chapter 20

Rachel stood outside Jonah's door holding his breakfast tray, waiting for a break in Abby's conversation with their cousin so she wouldn't interrupt. But when she heard her *schweschder* say they didn't share the same *daed,* she felt like she couldn't breathe. And when she heard her cousin ask Abby to run away with him to Florida, Rachel had heard enough and threw the breakfast tray to floor, storming down the hall to pack her things. She was angry and had to get away from Abby. She wouldn't stick around and watch her *schweschder* hurt her or the rest of the *familye* by selfishly running away again. She had to get home—to get her *mamm* to fix things somehow.

When Abby reached the doorway to Jonah's room, she found a tray on the floor, a ceramic bowl full of oatmeal had split down the middle; oatmeal spilling from the gap. A puddle of orange juice glittered with bits of the broken glass spread across the middle of the path between her and her *schweschder,* who'd ducked inside the spare room and slammed the door shut.

Abby's heart pounded in perfect rhythm to the sound of horses hooves coming from outside. Jonah had a visitor. Scrambling to pick up the mess, Abby wondered just how much of her conversation with Jonah that her *schweschder* had overheard. Perhaps staying here had not been her best idea yet, but Abby didn't trust herself anymore to make the right decision about this situation. How could she leave here with Jonah and try to have a normal life with him when this mess would forever be held over their heads? But on the other hand; how could she possibly turn down his offer?

Abby mopped up the spilled juice with the linen napkin. She could hear the kitchen door swing open and a voice call out. It was Caleb.

"We're up here," Abby called out. "Will you grab the broom near the door and bring it up to me?"

Caleb was soon up the stairs, broom in hand.

"What happened here?"

Abby grabbed the broom from him and began to clear the broken glass from the hallway. "Rachel dropped the tray. I'll have it cleaned up in no time."

From down the hall, the door to the spare room swung open forcefully, and Rachel stepped into the hallway, tears staining her red-rimmed eyes. "Why don't you tell him the truth? You and I both know I threw that tray down on purpose."

Caleb walked toward his distraught younger *schweschder.* "Why would you do such a thing?"

Rachel leered at Abby. "I'd tell you to ask your *schweschder,* except she isn't your *schweschder.*"

Caleb's eyes widened as he turned to Abby. "What is she saying?"

Tears filled Abby's eyes, and she found it difficult to breathe. "Rachel, I'm sorry. I never meant for you to find out this way. I'm still your *schweschder.*"

Rachel stormed down the hall toward them. "You're *half* right about that because you and I are only related by *mamm;* you and Caleb aren't related at all. And neither are you and Jonah. I guess that's why you're planning on running off to Florida with him."

Abby couldn't face the looks from both of her siblings that seemed to cut right through her. She let the broom drop to the floor and ran down the stairs. Caleb called after her, but she grabbed her coat and ran out of Jonah's *haus.*

Caleb stepped over the mess of dishes and food that still littered the hallway, and turned to Rachel. "Get yours and Abby's things together. I'll be taking you home."

Rachel did as she was told.

Caleb walked into his cousin's room and closed the door. He crossed over to the bed and looked Jonah in the eye for several minutes before composing his emotions enough to speak. "Are you planning on running off to Florida with Abby?"

Jonah felt vulnerable lying flat on his back, and tried to push himself up on his elbows. When he'd managed to position himself so he could lean his back against the headboard of the bed, he closed his eyes momentarily until the severe pounding in his head let up a little. "I asked her to go with me. I'd like to marry her. I love her. I always have. And now that she tells me we aren't really cousins after all, I won't let anything stop me from having the life I've dreamed of having with her for several years now."

Shivering, Caleb crossed to the open window and closed it. "What makes her think she isn't related to you or to me?"

Jonah winced against the pain in his head, and ignored the dizziness he felt from sitting upright. "She told me her real *daed* is an *Englischer* named Eddie Monroe. You don't share the same *daed* or *mamm* the way you thought you did. After your *daed* married Abby's *mamm,* you became siblings my marriage only. Since I'm *your* cousin, I'm not hers. Which means we are free to marry."

Caleb collapsed into a chair in the corner of Jonah's room. If what his cousin was saying had any truth to it; that meant his *daed* had been lying to him for the past fifteen years. Unless *he* didn't know the truth either. Was it possible he only *thought* he was

Abby's *daed* all these years, and his *mamm*—Abby's *mamm,* had lied to all of them?

Caleb turned to Jonah. "How long has Abby known?"

"She found out five years ago. That's why she left the community."

It was obvious to Caleb that he'd misjudged Abby. It was Abby's *mamm* he needed to confront.

Chapter 21

Abby wandered around in the snow, the wind stinging her cheeks with tiny ice crystals. Before she realized, she found herself standing before the set of mulberry trees beside the school house. Funny how she always ended up here—where it all started.

Lowering herself onto the snow-covered swing that hung from one of the trees, Abby was reminded that there were no students in attendance. They'd been out of school for the past few days after the teacher, Nettie Graber, had fallen on the icy steps and broken her right leg and her left arm. The replacement, Nettie's niece, Katie, was due in from Nappanee next week.

Abby relished the solitude, but wished for Jonah to be by her side. She struggled to understand how things could have gotten so far out of control, but this was a perfect example of how one little lie could hurt so many people. This was too big for her to continue to push aside. She wasn't even sure how she would have the strength of spirit to forgive her *mamm*. She thought she had forgiven her, but new pain and anger plagued her, leaving her wondering if she'd ever be able to get past this hurt.

The look in Caleb's eyes were of judgment—for her—even though Abby was just as much a victim of the aftermath of the lie as he and Rachel were. Did he blame her for what her *mamm* had done? As the sound of a buggy neared, she looked up, noting that it was her *Onkel* Seth. She ran to the road to greet him.

Seth signaled the mare to stop when Abby approached. "You look frozen to the bone. What are you doing out here? You must have three inches of snow in your hair." he reached down and assisted her into the buggy and handed her a lap quilt. Despite being out of the wind, Abby continued to shiver, her teeth chattering so much she couldn't speak.

Seth clicked to mare, and they began to move slowly along the slushy road. "From the look of you, I'd guess you could use someone to talk to. I was on my way over Jonah's place so I could talk to you about something, but I don't want to add to your burdens."

Abby pulled the other lap quilt around her shoulders. "I could actually use the distraction. Maybe if I can help someone else solve their troubles, it might take my mind off of my own."

Seth smiled. "Fair enough. Do you want me to drop you back at Jonah's?"

Abby shook her head. "Caleb and Rachel are there now. Take me to the bakery. Maybe I could help *Aenti* Lillian for a while."

"That's kind of what I wanted to talk to you about. Lillian won't go back to the bakery. We've been to the B&B the past three days and she refuses to meet Ellie. I'm worried the girl is going to go back to Ohio and change her mind about letting us adopt her *boppli.*"

"I'm not going to tell you that worry is a sin because I'm guilty of doing an awful lot of worrying myself lately. But it seems to me that if you want *Aenti* to do anything, you have to let it be *her* idea. Or at least let her *think* that it's her idea."

Seth steered the horse toward the bakery. "I'm not sure I follow that line of thinking."

"Well you know the expression, *you can lead a horse to water, but you can't make him drink?* It's sort of the same principle. When you go to the B&B, don't ask her visit with Ellie. Wait for her to decide on her own. As for the bakery, you'll have to bring her, but not ask her to bake anything. If you bring her for a visit with me, she will naturally pitch in to help, and it will be *her* idea, not because either of us has asked her to do it."

Seth set the break. "That makes sense. Will you be here for a while? I'd like to bring her by today. It's still early enough that the two of you could have a pretty productive day. I could have her here in less than thirty minutes. What you do think?"

Abby stepped out of her *onkel's* buggy. "I think that's a *gut* idea. Tell her I need someone to talk to; that will get her here. And *Gott* knows I need to talk."

"I'll be back with her as soon as I can."

"*Denki, Onkel* Seth."

Abby turned to leave, but swung back around. "One more thing…maybe *Aenti* Lillian needs a simple reminder of why you married her in the first place."

Seth smiled. "*Denki,* Abby. I know just the thing."

Abby watched him drive off, and then turned toward Jonah's *haus.* Noting that Caleb's buggy was still there, she knew Jonah was in capable hands for the time being. And knowing her *bruder* would not leave his cousin alone in his weakened state, Abby let herself into the bakery, grateful she'd had the key in her coat pocket.

Tying on a clean apron, Abby was eager to have something to occupy her hands and her mind. Before long, she was humming her favorite hymn, and mixing enough batter for several tins of cinnamon muffins. She intended to send some home with Caleb, and some with her *aenti.*

But given the circumstances, there was no way Caleb would tolerate her staying with Jonah—not even with a chaperone. She wouldn't abandon Jonah in his time of need, even if it meant having to speak to the Bishop. She guessed that her *bruder* was making arrangements to stay overnight with Jonah, and Abby would be agreeable with that, as long as no one stood in the way of her spending the day with him. She would get her *aenti* to come back to the bakery for a few days, until Jonah was back on his feet again.

But there was still the matter of Jonah's question.

Chapter 22

By the time Lillian was dropped off at the bakery, she was nearly frantic with worry for Abby. The way her husband described finding her crying in the school yard was enough to break her heart for her niece. She had an idea Abby's troubles involved Jonah in some capacity, and she was the person to help.

Her husband promised to come back in two hours to pick her up after he went into town for a few supplies. Lillian was looking forward to a nice talk with Abby, but more than that, she was eager to be at the bakery again. Truth be told, she missed it. The feel of flour between her fingers, the smell of freshly baked bread. She was so happy that for the first time in nearly two months her husband hadn't tried to convince her to go back to the bakery, she found herself wanting to be there more than ever.

Walking inside, the jingling of the bells on the door alerted her niece, who was hard at work, that she'd come to help her. Grabbing an apron from a peg on the back wall of the kitchen, Lillian felt ready to dive into baking.

"I'd say by the amount of things you're preparing, you're either planning on opening the bakery for the day, or this problem of yours is bigger than I can help you with."

Abby looked up her with sad eyes. "Maybe a little of both."

Lillian grabbed a section of bread dough and began to knead. "How's Jonah? He must be feeling a lot better if you're here instead of at his *haus.*"

Abby sighed. "Caleb and Rachel are with him. They're both upset with me. I've really made a mess of things."

Lillian covered her bread dough with cheesecloth and set it aside. "Tell me what happened."

"I told Jonah the truth about us not being real cousins, and he asked me to go to Florida with him. I'm not sure I can do that, even though it's probably the only chance we will have of leading a normal life together."

Lillian gave an encouraging smile. "Is that what you want to do?"

Abby pulled a tray of heart-shaped cookies from the oven. "I will miss my *familye*—especially

Rachel. She's the only *schweschder* I have. When I first came back, she was distant and didn't trust me. Now she trusted me and I let her down again. She was standing outside of Jonah's door and heard our conversation. She's upset that he asked me to go to Florida with him."

"What about Caleb? What did he say about it?"

"*Ach, Aenti,* Rachel had already told him before I had a chance to explain it to him. You should have seen the look on his face. He blames me for what my *mamm* did. I don't want him to have anger and unforgiveness for me or for my *mamm.* I remember when we first met how much he wanted a new *mamm.* He was so happy that we had joined him and his *daed* to make a *familye.* But now I think he wishes we hadn't."

Lillian hugged Abby, who'd begun to cry. "Don't say such things. It might take a little time for the shock of it to sink in, but he will remember the love he has for both of you. Caleb hasn't forgotten what it felt like to lose his own *mamm,* and how excited he was when your *mamm* became his *mamm* too. Just give it some time."

Abby wiped her tears with the edge of her apron. "I don't think I have much time left. Jonah is planning to leave in just a few days. If I don't go with him, I fear I may never see him again."

Lillian grabbed the bowl of pink icing and began to spread it on the cooled cookies. "Have you talked to your *mamm* yet?"

Abby placed another batch of heart-shaped cookies into the oven. "I gave her a chance to do the right thing and she said she couldn't do it. She isn't going to go to the Bishop, so I guess I have no other choice but to go to Florida with Jonah."

Lillian choked up at the thought of it. "If you leave, I will miss you, and so will your *familye*. I know how much your *mamm* missed you when you left five years ago. She cried a lot. She put up a brave front, but I could see the sadness in her eyes."

"I know how much it hurt her, so why doesn't that make her want to do whatever it takes to make this right? Why do you suppose she won't go to the Bishop? She mentioned it might be worse for my *daed* if she did that. Do you think Jacob could be excommunicated for this?"

Lillian bit into one of the heart-shaped cookies. "These are so *gut*. You've made a lot of progress with your baking skills."

Setting the cookie down, Lillian chose her words carefully. "Bishop Troyer is a very understanding and lenient *mann,* but your *daed* is the head of the *familye,* and that means it is his responsibility to uphold the bylaws of the community. What your *mamm* did, well…he went along with it, and that could mean strict discipline for him."

Abby swallowed a lump in her throat. "He's been a *gut daed* to me. Better than my real *daed* could have ever been. I don't want him to be hurt in all of this. I think he was just trying to be honorable and do what was right in the situation. My *mamm* is the one that put Jacob's name on my birth certificate. She is the one that didn't speak up and tell the truth from the very beginning. I know she was only trying to protect me, but her decision has hurt me more than it could have ever protected me."

The jingling of the bells on the front door moved the two of them out of the kitchen. Rachel stood at the doorway with her eyes cast downward.

"Caleb sent me down here to get you and bring you back to Jonah's *haus.*"

"How did he know I was here?"

"He could smell the cookies. He said to bring some with you."

Abby smiled. That was a *gut* sign. If he wanted cookies, that meant he was ready to talk to her. If only she could say the same for Rachel.

Chapter 23

Abby didn't waste any time gathering a dozen cookies and putting them into a box to take with her to Jonah's *haus.*

"I hate to leave you here all alone, *Aenti.*"

Lillian shooed her with her hand. "Being here was just what I needed to feel better. It might take some time for me to get back to my old routine, but I feel ready to try. Besides, your *Onkel* Seth will be back here in about an hour to pick me up. I think we might have to go around the community and gift some of these cookies and muffins and bread, but I'm alright with that. Go and talk to your *bruder,* and try to reconnect with Rachel. She needs her big *schweschder* right now. She's at that delicate age where she's working on becoming an adult, and she really needs you."

Abby hugged her *aenti.* "I know. She's the biggest reason I don't want to leave. I never had an older *schweschder.* You were the closest thing I had to that, and I'll never forget how much it meant to me to have you around. I can't take that away from her."

Lillian smiled. "Now you're thinking straight. Pray some more about this. *Gott* will make things right. Maybe not in the way you see it, but in the way that is best for everyone."

Abby gathered the cookies and muffins and headed out into the snow toward Jonah's *haus,* hope filling her that *Gott* would make things right.

Lillian pulled the last of the loaves of fresh bread out of the oven and set them aside to cool. She'd finished most of the cleanup, and wrapped most of the loaves of bread. She'd heard a wagon pull into the parking lot a few minutes before, and tried to hurry so she wouldn't make her husband wait. Just a few more dishes, and she would be done. If she knew her husband, he was probably talking to the horse rather than coming inside and talking to the women-folk. He had no idea Abby had left, but Lillian giggled at the thought of her husband talking to the horse anyway. A little cold weather and snow wouldn't hurt him. Besides, she only had about ten minutes worth of work to finish. She knew if he got cold enough, he'd come in and stand by the stove to warm up. In the meantime, she had bread pans to wash.

ｏｏｏｏｏ

Seth knew his *fraa* would stay and talk even after she heard his buggy pull into the lot behind the bakery. She knew him well enough to know he'd choose talking to his horse over being a third party to women's conversation. This, he knew, would afford him the time to set up the surprise he had for her, hoping to break through her shell of sadness. Thankful for the continuous snow, Seth set to work on the bottom of the snowman. He hoped he'd have enough time to finish it before Lillian came outside, but she knew he'd go inside the bakery to get her if he got too cold.

The snow was packing very nicely, making quick work of the bottom portion. Next, he rolled the middle, making sure it was smaller, but not so large that he wouldn't be able to lift it onto the bottom. Seth pushed the large bottom portion so it was centered with the large window in the front of the bakery. Next, he pushed the middle up onto the base, and quickly rolled a head for it. Plopping the head on top, he was satisfied with the height.

Almost as tall as me.

Pulling the stones from his pocket, he pushed them into the head to make eyes. He hoped Lillian would know that the stones came from the keepsake spice box he'd given her five years ago for her birthday. He hoped this gesture would remind his *fraa* of how much he loved and cherished her.

Locating a couple of fallen twigs from the large maple tree in the lot, Seth pushed them into the sides of the middle for arms. Next he snapped off a few smaller branches and broke them into short pieces to make a large smile on the snowman.

When he was satisfied the snowman was finished, he stood proudly beside him and waited patiently for Lillian to exit the bakery.

Lillian took the baked goods out the back door of the bakery and placed them in the back of the buggy. Seth was nowhere around. Wondering if he'd gone in the front door, which would have been unlocked, she went back inside to check for him and make sure she locked the front door before leaving. Once inside, she called out her husband's name, but he didn't answer. Thinking it was strange, she went to the front of the store to lock the front door before searching for Seth.

Stopping short of the front door, Lillian spotted her husband standing next to a large snowman similar to the one they'd made on their first date. Tears welled up in her eyes, and a lump formed in her throat. She opened the door and ran to him, jumping into his waiting arms. He spun her around before setting her down.

"I can't believe you did this for me. Are those the same rocks from the original snowman?"

Seth took off his gloves and cupped her face in his hands. "As a matter of fact, they are. I wanted you to know how much I love you…how much I will always love you."

Seth pressed his lips to hers and kissed her, gently sweeping his cold lips across her warm ones.

Lillian leaned into his kiss with a passion she hadn't felt for a while. "I love you too, Seth. Can we go to the B&B? I'm ready to meet Ellie."

Seth let out a whoop, and picked her up and twirled her around again. He hadn't felt this happy in a while, and it felt *gut.*

Chapter 24

Abby hung up her coat on the peg in Jonah's kitchen. She could hear faint voices from upstairs, and decided to place the cookies on a plate and bring a pitcher of milk with her before going up to greet the three of them. She dreaded having to tell Jonah she wouldn't be able to go to Florida with him right now, but hoped he would wait for her to straighten things out here with her *familye* first. She hoped he would understand and be willing to wait for her.

As she neared the top step, Abby heard her siblings laughing. That was a *gut* sign. She stood in the doorway and waited for a break in the laughter.

Caleb held his hand out to her. "Abby, *kume.* We need to talk."

Abby walked timidly toward them, noting that Jonah was sitting upright and looking like the color had returned to his face. She sat in the chair that her *bruder* had gotten up from, and waited for him to have his say.

Caleb sat on the edge of the windowsill. "I've had a couple of hours for your news to sink in, and I just want to say I'm sorry for the way I reacted—or didn't react. I'm also sorry for our little talk we had the other day in the barn. Why didn't you tell me the truth then?"

"It wasn't my truth to tell. It doesn't matter anyway. It's not like it would have made any difference. There isn't anything any of us can do about it."

She turned to Jonah then. "I'm sorry, Jonah, but I can't go with you to Florida right now. I know I'm grown up, but that doesn't mean I can run away from my *familye* again. I did it once, and it was the biggest mistake I've ever made. The longer I was away, the easier it was to stay away, and I don't want to do that again. I've missed too much time with my little *schweschder* already."

Rachel walked over and placed her hand on Abby's shoulder. "I want you to go to Florida."

Abby's heart sank. Did her *schweschder* want to be rid of her?

"Why, Rachel?"

"You're my *schweschder,* and I love you. I'll miss you terribly, but you must go so you can be happy. You can't do that if you stay here. Seeing you here taking care of Jonah is the happiest I've ever seen you."

Caleb stood up. "Rachel's right. I'd be honored if you'd marry my cousin. I can't think of a better *mann* for you. Go. Be happy in Florida."

Tears filled Abby's eyes as she looked over at Jonah. "Are you sure we can't try to stay here?"

Jonah had a mixture of emotion showing in his eyes. "I don't see any other way for us to be together. If you go with me, I promise to make you happy."

Abby reached over and placed her hand in his.

"You already do."

Caleb walked over to the tray of cookies and milk and started pouring the milk into the glasses. "Then let's celebrate. The smell of these cookies has been making my mouth water since you walked into the room with them."

Abby wiped a tear from the corner of her eye.

"How am I going to break the news to *Mamm* and *Daed?*"

Caleb handed her a glass of milk and a cookie on a napkin. "I'll help you. I think it might be easier if they know I support your decision. I'm curious about something though. Did *Daed* know about this all along?"

Abby gulped down the milk in her mouth. "I'm afraid so. In all fairness to him, he went along with it to protect *Mamm's* honor. His heart was in the right place, but neither of them had time to think it through. Bishop Troyer was a lot more strict back then. He pressed for the marriage more than either of them."

"I suppose it was what was best for everyone at the time, given the circumstances. That doesn't make it right for *your* situation. I stand by what I said. I think your best chance of happiness is to start over in the community in Florida."

Abby smiled. "*Denki,* Caleb. As far as I'm concerned, no matter what the truth is, you'll always be my *bruder,* and Jacob will always be my *daed.*"

Caleb hugged her lightly. "In my heart, you'll always be my *schweschder.*"

Caleb offered Jonah a cookie and he turned it down. "I'm not sure my stomach can handle any solid food yet, no matter how *gut* they are."

Caleb stepped back over to the window and leaned against the sill again. "There's one more issue we need to address."

He looked at Abby sternly. "I will stay here with Jonah overnight while he's recovering, and you can take care of him during the day. That is if Rachel is in agreement to act as chaperone."

Rachel and Abby nodded in agreement.

"Doctor Davis should be here soon. While he's here, we can go home and talk to *Mamm* and *Daed.* I've had Rachel pack your things. You can come back in the morning."

Abby was happy for her sibling's help with Jonah. While she couldn't wait to start her life with Jonah in Florida, she dreaded having to tell her parents.

Chapter 25

Abby pulled the buggy into Becca's yard. After the heart-wrenching talk she'd had with her *familye* the night before, she was ready for something cheerful. She couldn't wait to see the new *boppli,* and give her the news of Jonah's recovery. Levi let her in and led her to the bedroom where Becca was cuddling her new bundle.

She approached Becca quietly, making sure she didn't wake the *boppli.* "*Gudemariye, wie gehts?*"

Becca sighed. "Still pretty tired, but I'm happy. How's my *bruder?* Is he giving you a hard time, or is he being a *gut* patient?"

Abby's cheeks heated. "He's doing much better, but I didn't stay with him last night. My *bruder* took over watching him at night, and I'll be watching over him for the next few days until the doctor gives him permission to be out of bed."

"Would you like to hold the *boppli?*"

Abby eagerly held out her arms and reached for little Adam. She cradled him close, enjoying the new *boppli* smell. *Boppli's* always had such a sweet scent that nothing could compare to.

Becca straightened herself in the bed, trying to get comfortable. "I hear your *Aenti* Lillian is adopting a *boppli.*"

Abby cooed at little Adam. "They haven't decided for certain I think. But I'm hoping they will. I think it will be *gut* for them—and for the *boppli.*"

Concern furrowed Becca's brow. "I'll be honest with you; when I heard what happened to your *aenti,* I told Levi I wanted the doctor in attendance for Adam's birth. I wasn't comfortable having just the midwife here. And it's nothing against Miriam. I just wanted everything to go smoothly."

"From what Doctor Davis tells me, you aren't the only one who feels that way. He's had several requests for deliveries in the past month."

Abby handed the *boppli* back to Becca, and sat in the chair by her bedside. "There's something I need to tell you before you hear it from someone else."

Alarm crossed Becca's face faster than a lightning strike. "Is there something you haven't told me about my *bruder?*"

Abby held up a hand to stop her grief. "No, he's going to be sore for a few days, but doc says he'll recover. But this does have to do with Jonah—and me."

Becca let a gasp escape her lips. "Did the two of you kiss again? Oh no; by the look on your face, I'd say you did. Abby, don't you know the two of you are going to get yourselves excommunicated."

Abby couldn't help but fan her heated cheeks. "I'm not your cousin. I'm not Jonah's cousin. And Jacob Yoder isn't my real *daed.*" She'd spoken it all so fast she didn't even stop to take a breath.

"Slow down, Abby. You're telling me you're not related to me or my *bruder?*"

Abby swallowed down the lump that tried to bring tears to her eyes. "It's a long story, and I don't really want to reveal the details right now, but it's true."

"What do you plan on doing? Will you go to the Bishop and tell him?"

Abby felt a tear roll down her cheek. "It's not that simple. If I go to the Bishop, it will bring shame to my *mamm* and *daed.* It could get *them* excommunicated. They are getting older, and they need the community. But Jonah and I can start over in another community. He suggested Florida since your *mamm's bruder* is there and he could help us."

Tears filled Becca's eyes. "Florida is so far away. Jonah is the only *familye* I have left. How long have the two of you been planning this?"

Abby suddenly wished she would have waited for Jonah to have this conversation with Becca. They'd been friends for fifteen years, but she and

Jonah had been *familye* for a lot longer. She couldn't bear to see Becca hurt, but she didn't think she could wait until the end of the week and surprise her with the news at the last minute.

"Jonah has been planning it for a week now. I thought he would have told you by now."

Becca sniffled. "He mentioned he'd like to go, but I thought he was only thinking about it. I never imagined he'd consider really going. I want little Adam to grow up knowing his *Onkel* Jonah. It breaks my heart that they haven't even met yet."

"The Doctor practically had to strap him to his bed to keep him from getting up and coming to see you. He feels just awful that he can't be here. And I'm sorry for telling you all of this; I thought you knew Jonah was leaving at the end of next week."

Becca placed the *boppli* over her shoulder to burp him. "Will you be going with him?"

Abby paused before answering, hoping to gain some composure. "He asked me to go. At first, I told him I couldn't go with him, but Caleb and Rachel talked me into it. And when I talked to my *mamm* last night, it was apparent that she had no intention of going to the Bishop on my behalf, so I've decided to go. It's the only chance we have for having a normal life together. We plan to marry when we arrive in Florida."

"I'm going to miss your wedding?"

Abby managed a weak smile. "I suppose it's only fair since I missed your wedding. We will want you to visit once we've settled into the new community."

Becca sniffled some more. "All this time I thought you were my cousin, and now you're going to be my *schweschder*-in-law. It's funny how things work out."

Abby was glad Becca was taking the news as well as she was. Deep down, Abby hoped they didn't have to go. Was it too unreasonable for her to hope that her *mamm* would save her from having to leave her *familye* and her best friend again?

Please Gott, we're going to need a miracle.

Chapter 26

Lizzie took hot *kaffi* out to the barn to Jacob, who had been making slow progress with the morning chores in Caleb's absence. As she trudged through the deep snow, she pulled her coat close to guard against the wind, wondering if spring would ever come.

Opening the barn door, she searched for her husband, dreading the moment when their eyes would meet, for he would surely know her mood just by looking at her.

Jacob reached for the *kaffi*, "Is something weighing on your mind? You've been quiet since last night just after Caleb left for Jonah's *haus*."

Lizzie knew it was time to discuss this with her husband, so why was it so difficult for her to say the words? Perhaps it was because she already knew what she needed to do, and she needed Jacob's approval.

"The *kinner* had a talk with me yesterday late afternoon, and I need to discuss it with you. I wanted them to include you in the conversation, but they thought it was best if they spoke to me alone first."

Jacob leaned against the pitchfork he'd been using to clean out the stalls. "This sounds serious."

Lizzie lowered herself onto a milking stool and cupped her forehead in her hands, pausing for a deep breath. "I've made a mess of my life from the very day I left this community when I was eighteen, and it's still affecting my *dochder* negatively. I made a mistake in judgment by trusting a young, *Englisch buwe* and I'm still paying for it all these years later."

Jacob set the pitchfork against the stall and went to his *fraa's* side. "Lizzie, we've talked about this before, and you know that *Gott* brought forth the miracle of Abby when you strayed from His path. *Gott* always has a way of turning the bad things we do into *gut*—especially since He knows your heart is in Him. We might stray from the path, but He always brings us back to Him."

Lizzie began to get choked up. "I know that, but because of my sin, *Gott* has taken her from me once already. And now, it's happening again."

"What are you talking about?"

Lizzie began to cry. "Our *dochder* is planning on leaving the community again and I have the power to stop her, but I don't know if I have the strength to do it."

Jacob felt suddenly weak, lowering himself onto a fresh bale of hay across from Lizzie. "Why is she leaving? Is it because of Jonah?"

Lizzie wiped her tear-dampened face. "They're planning to go to Florida together so they can marry there."

If Jacob hadn't already been sitting, he'd have fallen over from the shock of it. "They plan to get married? Why didn't she come to me? Do you think she's never really felt I was her *daed?*"

Lizzie shrugged. "If I would have waited to tell her the truth back then until you could be there to help me break the news to her, I believe we could have spared all of us the pain of her leaving the first time. It's a regret I have to live with. But this time, I want to do the right thing so I don't keep living with regret. I have to go to the Bishop and accept whatever consequences there are—for the sake of my *dochder's* happiness."

"I think that's wise. But I shoulder the blame for how far this has gotten out of control. I should have spoken up from the very beginning." He turned to Lizzie. "Don't misunderstand me. I still would have married you, but I would have never gone along with this lie that has been eating away at our *familye* all these years."

Lizzie looked at her husband sorrowfully. Her lie to protect her *dochder* had been the very thing that hurt her most. And her husband still loved her in spite of it all. She didn't feel she deserved that love, but she intended to earn it. And if Abby would ever consider forgiving her, she had to make it right, and she had to do it immediately.

"Maybe we should break the news to the rest of the *kinner* before we go to the Bishop."

Lizzie shook her head. "Caleb and Rachel already know, and they're taking it better than I expected they would. They actually support Abby's decision to go to Florida. I don't think Liam knows, but he's always off somewhere with his cousins and friends. He would be gone from sun-up to sun-down if we let him. I guess we need to track him down and have a *familye* discussion about all of this. If we can keep Abby here, and make it so she and Jonah can be married here, then I am willing to accept whatever my fate is here in the community. But Abby deserves to stay here if that's what she wants."

Lizzie wondered how such an innocent lie could have gotten so far out of control that it had nearly torn her *familye* apart. Her intentions in the beginning were to hide her *dochder* from the *mann* who had taken advantage of her in her youth and stolen her innocence. A *mann* who was a dangerous drug addict and a criminal for all she knew. She should have told Abby the truth after Eddie's death. Instead, she had allowed her own selfish desires to cloud her judgment of what was right. She had put her own wants before those of her *dochder,* and it was her *dochder* who was paying for her mistakes.

All of that was about to change.

Lizzie could not let another day go by without bringing the truth forward once and for all. She would stand before the Bishop and confess, even if meant she would be excommunicated.

Chapter 27

By the time Abby reached Jonah's *haus,* she was emotionally drained. Rachel had been fairly quiet the entire trip. She was grateful her *schweschder* had agreed to stay outside at Becca's *haus* and play with the kittens in the barn while she talked with her in private. It wasn't that she'd said anything Rachel didn't already know, but she didn't want her *schweschder* to hear any unpleasant conversation if there had been any. Thankfully, Becca had taken the news well. Abby suspected she was far too happy with her new *boppli* for much of anything to bother her for the time-being, but she welcomed the distraction nonetheless.

Abby left her horse outside in the yard at Jonah's *haus*, knowing Caleb would tend to the mare before he left. She was eager to see how Jonah was feeling after not being able to stay with him during the night. When she entered the kitchen, Jonah was sitting at the table, fully dressed and wearing the grin that she loved so much.

"*Gudemariye,* Jonah. You look *wunderbaar.* Should you be out of bed though?"

Jonah smiled from ear to ear, but Abby could see he still fought back pain.

"Don't worry so much about me. I'm strong. And the doc gave me permission to be up. As a matter of fact, he even gave me permission to get a little fresh air."

Abby smiled. "That's *wunderbaar.*"

Jonah reached for Abby's hand. "We haven't taken a buggy ride for a long time. What do you say we do that now while I still have the energy?"

Abby furrowed her brow. "Are you sure the jostling of the buggy won't hurt your head? Maybe we should just take a little walk instead."

Jonah squeezed her hand and smiled. "Where I want to go is a little too far to walk. If we go slowly I'll be fine."

Abby's pulse raced, and she smiled knowingly. She knew where he wanted to take her, and she was eager to go.

Abby's heart skipped a beat when the familiar set of mulberry trees came into view. Jonah had insisted on driving, and she'd cuddled next to him to stay warm. They'd taken many forbidden buggy rides together, but this one seemed more special than all the rest. This one seemed more like an official date.

Jonah stepped down carefully from the buggy, and then held out his hand to assist Abby. She thought he had never looked more handsome than he did now. His smile showed the slightest of dimples at each side of his cheeks, his blue eyes sparkled in the bright sunshine. With the bandage on his head covered by his hat, it was easy to pretend everything was alright—especially since he didn't let his pain wipe the smile from his face.

They walked over and stood beneath the mulberry tree where they'd shared their first kiss. Jonah pulled her into his arms and kissed her temples. He knew he shouldn't risk holding her and kissing her out in the open, but the school was vacant, and there was no one around but the two of them. She felt comfortable in his arms, like she had always meant to be there. He breathed in the scent of fresh lilac soap; a hint of cinnamon that lingered on the collar of her coat. The lonely void he'd felt for so many years all melted away in this one embrace. He never knew love could feel this freeing. He unbuttoned his coat, wrapping it around Abby as he held her close. Her warm breath seeped through his shirt as she rested her head against his chest. He didn't want to let her go, but he'd brought her here for a reason, and he needed to speak his mind before his energy drained.

"You know I always hoped we'd be married here beneath these trees. But since we can't, I figured at the very least, you deserved a proper proposal. And what better place than right here where it all began."

Abby wasn't willing to lift her head from his chest just yet. She needed to hear the soothing beat of his heart to validate the moment—to ensure the reality of it. Jonah's hand held her there at the base of her neck, his fingers gently raking through the loose strands of her hair. It sent twinges of desire through her, making her momentarily forget the riskiness of their actions.

Jonah tucked his hand under Abby's chin and lifted until her lips met his. The warmth of her mouth on his, and the sweetness of her shallow breaths made him wish they were already married. He gently held her away from him, and knelt before her. Taking her hands in his, he looked up into her glistening eyes.

"Abby, I've loved you since the day we first met, but I fell in love with you the first time I kissed you under this very tree. Marry me so I can enjoy your love and your sweet kisses I can't live without. Continue to be my best friend, and become my helpmate until death parts us."

Abby's lower lip quivered with joy, tears filling her eyes.

"I will marry you, but only if we are married here, under the mulberry tree."

Jonah stood up abruptly, the pain in his head causing him to groan under his breath. "That's not possible, Abby and we both know it. There is no way

Bishop Troyer is going to marry us when he thinks we are first cousins. If we were second cousins, we wouldn't have a problem, but since your *familye's* lie is preventing us from marrying in the community, we must wait until we go to Florida."

Abby took Jonah's hands in hers. "Just the other day you said that even *Gott* Himself couldn't make us so we weren't cousins, but He did! Let's not be hasty and give up on that miracle we've been hoping for. *Gott* will make this right for us, and we *will* be married here."

Abby was right, but Jonah still found it difficult to trust in what he wanted most—to have her as his *fraa,* and to be able to live in this community with her.

Abby felt a mixture of sadness and elation as they left the mulberry tree. She was engaged, but her heart ached at the thought of not being able to marry Jonah under their tree.

Chapter 28

Seth steered the horse into the curved driveway in front of the B&B. It would be their second meeting with Ellie, and he was hopeful that she was going to grant them adoption rights for her *boppli*.

Seth squeezed Lillian's hand. "Are you ready to go ask her if she's made up her mind?"

Lillian looked at her husband through tearful eyes.

"What if she says no? I'm not sure I can handle that."

Seth pulled her into his arms. "We prayed about it, and now it's up to *Gott*. I believe He put Ellie in our path for a reason. We have to trust that."

Lillian wiped her tears. "You're right. If it's *Gotte's wille,* we will be that *boppli's familye.*"

Seth kissed his *fraa* full on the mouth. "I love you."

Lillian kissed him back and couldn't help but smile. "I love you too."

"*Denki* for opening your heart to Ellie. You're going to be a *gut mamm.*"

"And you're going to be a *gut daed.* I'm really happy *Gott* brought Ellie into our lives. I know *Gott* can't bring back our little *buwe,* but maybe He's giving us the opportunity to help a *boppli* who needs a *familye* just as much as we want to be his or her *familye.*"

Seth and Lillian stomped their feet on the porch of the B&B so they wouldn't track snow in on *Aenti* Bess's hardwood floors. She worked hard to keep the country charm atmosphere in the B&B, and the freshly polished floors were difficult to maintain in the winter.

Bess suddenly rushed down the stairs pretty fast for a woman her age. "I need your help up there, Lillian. Ellie's in labor. *Boppli's* coming fast. I'm not sure the doctor is going to get here in time."

Lillian's pulse raced at the thought of it. What could she do? She wasn't a midwife. Fear coursed through her when another thought crossed her mind. If Ellie was having the *boppli* now, then it was possible she was about to become a new *mamm.*

Please Gott, let Ellie bless me and Seth with this boppli. It's my heart's desire to be this boppli's familye.

Upstairs, Lillian felt awkward and out of place. She didn't know what she was doing there, except that *Aenti* Bess had told her on the way up to the room that Ellie had voiced that she wanted her to be there when she had the *boppli.* Lillian hoped her nervousness wouldn't be misinterpreted by Ellie as not wanting to adopt the *boppli.*

"What do you want me to do, *Aenti?*"

Bess took charge of the room. She was no stranger to delivering *bopplies,* even though she'd never established herself as an official midwife.

"Do you remember the breathing I taught you so you could give birth to your own *boppli?*"

The mention of Lillian's *boppli* didn't make her cry this time because she was too preoccupied with helping Ellie. "*Jah.*"

Bess prepared clean towels and a small quilt. "Stay near her head and help her breathe through this, just like I showed you."

Lillian turned to Ellie and panted with her through a long contraction. When it was over, Ellie whined a little and asked for a cool cloth on her forehead. Lillian went to the other side of the room where a basin had been set up along with a large pitcher full of fresh water. She dampened a cloth and quickly returned to Ellie's side, who'd begun another strong contraction.

"Where's Melanie? Why isn't she here?"

Bess draped fresh linens over Ellie in preparation for the birth. "She went into town for some things about an hour ago. Ellie's water broke and the labor has progressed very quickly for a first *boppli*. She's nearly ready to start pushing."

Ellie pushed the pillow out of the way and propped herself on her elbows. "I think I've been having these contractions for a few hours. They were so light earlier that I just thought it was regular aches and pains the same I've had for the last few months. It didn't start to really get strong until my water broke. Oh…here comes another one."

Ellie braced herself, finding it difficult to follow Lillian's lead with the breathing. She felt a strong urge to push, and began to bear down a little.

"Don't push yet, Ellie. It's not quite time yet. Breathe through the contraction."

Ellie threw her head back. "I can't do this anymore. It hurts."

Ellie let out a scream. "Make it stop. Please."

Lillian tried to get her to focus, but it wasn't easy.

"Try to breathe with me, Ellie. You're almost there. You can do this."

Lillian took Ellie's hand, and felt her squeeze it, as she fell into the rhythm of breathing with her.

"On the next contraction, Ellie, I want you to push with all your strength." Bess had taken charge and decided it was time.

Lillian's heart pounded as she held Ellie's hand through the long push. She could see the *boppli's* head, and felt like her own head was being squeezed just as hard from the fear that tried to grip her.

The next push revealed a very pink little girl. She let out the sweetest little cry, almost breaking Lillian's heart for her. Bess cut the cord and placed her on the quilt, and then handed her over to Lillian.

"Take her over there and get her cleaned up, Lillian."

Instinctively, Lillian carried the squirming, crying *boppli* to the bureau and set her down to examine the perfection as she dipped a cloth in the water to wash her off. She'd held newborns before, but this one was special. This one could possibly be hers. Was it too bold to hope? She was possibly the most beautiful *boppli* Lillian had ever seen, and it scared her to think about how much she wanted to be her *mamm.*

She finished washing the perfect little newborn and wrapped her in a clean quilt, and then she walked over to the side of the bed where Bess was finishing up with the delivery. Lillian held her out to Ellie. "Do you want to hold her?"

Ellie put up a hand. "No. She's so small, I'm afraid I would break her. Besides, she's yours and Seth's. I signed the papers yesterday. You can take her home with you after you sign the papers. The lawyer is still here waiting on your signature."

Lillian's knees nearly gave out, and she stepped backward to sit in the chair in the corner of the room. She couldn't believe her ears. She cradled the *boppli* close to her and caressed her head. She was asleep from all the excitement.

Ellie smiled at her. "What are you going to name her?"

Lillian admired her new *boppli*. "I'm sure my husband would agree with me; I'd like to name her Ellie, if that's alright with you."

Ellie smiled again. "I'd like that very much."

Chapter 29

Lizzie was shaking as Jacob knocked on the Bishop's door. Was it too late to change her mind? It didn't matter because she knew she couldn't keep hurting her *familye*. The truth had been long overdue to come out into the open, and she was prepared to face it.

Gott, give me strength, and soften the Bishop's heart toward me and Jacob. Please don't let us be excommunicated.

Mrs. Troyer greeted them with a smile. "This is an unexpected surprise. Please *kume*. I will let my husband know we have company."

Jacob stopped her. "We aren't here for a visit. We need to see the Bishop for a confession."

Mrs. Troyer looked confused, but politely excused herself to get her husband.

Lizzie wrung her hands, despite the constant prayers that she repeated in her head.

Jacob felt unusually calm as Bishop Troyer entered the room. "We're here for a confession."

The Bishop's eyes darted back and forth between Jacob and Lizzie. "Both of you?"

Jacob and Lizzie nodded in unison.

Bishop Troyer motioned them toward the shaker furniture in the sitting room. "I've been wondering when you were going to come to me. Since it's been so many years, I wasn't sure if you were ever going to come forward."

Jacob and Lizzie looked at each other quizzically.

"You know why we're here?"

Bishop Troyer suppressed a grin. "You're here to tell me about Abby, and why I performed an impromptu wedding when it wasn't necessary. Am I right?"

Lizzie cleared her throat. "That's part of it. How much do you know?"

Bishop Troyer leaned forward in his chair. "Not much gets by me in my community. I knew the timing wasn't right for the two of you to have conceived Abby given how long you'd been gone from the community. And I knew your relationship had been a pure one from the amount of time you'd been allowed away from your *daed's* strict hold on you, Miss Elizabeth. Is that what the two of you came to tell me?"

The color drained from Lizzie's face as she nodded her answer to the Bishop's question. He'd known all along. "If you knew, why did you marry us that day?"

"I didn't see any reason not to. The fact that Hiram was pressing the issue didn't help either of you gather enough courage to tell the truth. I didn't think it would ever be a problem, but having both of you in the same community and widowed, well...I thought it was best to have you married once and for all."

Jacob felt both relief and annoyance with the situation. "There is a problem that has arisen out of this. Something neither of us could have foreseen."

Bishop Troyer put up a hand to stop Jacob from saying anymore. "Like I said. Not much gets by me unnoticed. I know about the situation with Abby and Jonah. I understand they're planning on going to Florida to be married, and you want them to be married here."

Lizzie shook her head. "*Jah*. We don't want her to have to leave the community. But we don't see how the community will accept a marriage between them since they know them as first cousins, even though they're not."

The Bishop gave them a serious look. "Are the two of you prepared to make a public announcement about this? You don't have to divulge personal information, but you will have to openly admit to the community that Abby is not related by blood to Jacob—that she isn't his *dochder*."

Jacob answered for both of them. "We're prepared to do that for our *dochder's* happiness."

Bishop Troyer stood. "You can make the announcement at the services tomorrow, and then I will agree to marry them."

Lizzie's eyes filled with tears. *Gott* had answered her prayers despite her sinful actions.

Chapter 30

Abby smiled as she stood before the Bishop, who'd positioned himself between the mulberry trees in the school yard, waiting for him to perform the marriage ceremony for her and Jonah. Snowflakes touched her pink cheeks, but she didn't care. She was finally marrying the only *mann* she could ever love. If it was possible, Jonah looked more handsome than ever on this snowy, February day. Wasn't this the month of love? Even if it wasn't for anyone else, it *was* for her.

Abby momentarily caught her *mamm's* loving glance. With that one look, Abby tried to convey all the love and gratitude she felt because of her *mamm's* brave confession. Abby knew it was because of *Gott's* love and her *mamm's* strength that she was standing here today, able to marry Jonah.

After a long talk with her *mamm* regarding the circumstances surrounding her conception, Abby finally understood why her *mamm* had felt the need to protect her in the manner in which she did. It was at that point that Abby stopped seeing her *mamm* as a liar, but as a strong woman who had endured a great hardship to protect her *dochder*. Abby admired her *mamm* for the strength it took for her to raise her alone in the *Englisch* world for the first ten years of her life. And for the courage it took for her *mamm* to return to the Amish community and face the consequences.

Abby quickly glanced at Jacob, who sat protectively at her *mamm's* side. She had a new respect for him, too. For accepting the responsibility of becoming her *daed,* and for protecting her from the harshness of her *Englisch* heritage.

Abby's eyes returned to Jonah, her love, and her future. She hoped that *Gott* would continue to bless her, and that she would be a strong *fraa* for Jonah, strong like her *mamm.*

Abby shivered a bit from the wind, but she was too excited to be here to care. There was no denying that a Florida wedding would have been warmer, but nothing could have warmed her heart more than being married to Jonah under the mulberry tree.

The End

Please enjoy the following sneak peek of Book 4, Amish Winter of Promises...

AMISH WINTER OF PROMISES
Book 4
Jacob's Daughter series
Sneak Peek

CHAPTER 1

"Help me! They're after me!"

The jingling of the bells on the front door of the bakery, and the frantic, female voice were enough to give Caleb's heart a jump start. From the spot under the kitchen sink, where he'd been trying to fix the leak, the noise startled him enough to make him hit his head on the copper pipe. Grabbing a rag to wipe his hands, he rushed to the front of the store to see what the urgency was.

As he rounded the corner of the kitchen, he could hear the dogs barking and snarling. They jumped at the front door, teeth exposed, as though they were after a prowler. From the corner of his eye, Caleb spotted the young woman, her arms full of books, a lunch pail dangling carelessly from her wrist. Her eyes were wide, her mouth agape, her ashen face glistening with a mist of perspiration. Caleb couldn't help but stare as he watched her gasp for breath as though she had been running for her life. Though she was safe inside the bakery, the dogs continued to make her jump every time they charged at the door.

Caleb turned fully toward her, a smile twisting up at the corners of his mouth. "Well that's your problem. I'd say they're after the salami and cheese in your lunch pail."

Katie Graber pushed her nose in the air. "I hardly see the humor in this. They tore the bottom of my dress, and nearly bit my leg off." She turned to the side to reveal the tear at the hem of her dress. "And how did you know what I have in my lunch pail?"

Caleb admired her as she pushed blonde hair behind her ear. "Because I'm in a bakery, but I can smell your lunch from way over here."

Katie straightened her disheveled coat and sighed at the torn hem of her dress. Her face was flush, and the blue of her eyes held a hint of fire in them. Agitation showed in her expression, and suspense hung in the air. Was she Nettie Graber's replacement at the school? From the look of it, Caleb didn't guess she was beginning her first day on the best of terms. If he wasn't so enamored by her pure beauty, he would have reveled in her agitation over the stray dogs.

Katie stiffened her chin. "I believe if I hadn't come in here those mongrels would have made a meal out of me!"

Caleb suppressed a smile. "Those mutts are harmless. They're hungry is all, and they could smell that salami in your lunch pail."

Katie looked toward the door, where the dogs continued to pace and whine. "It's none of your business what my lunch pail contains."

Rachel came in from the storeroom wiping her hands on her apron. "What's all the commotion out here?" She looked up at Katie and smiled. "Where are my manners? You must be the new school teacher. I'm Rachel Yoder. I run this bakery for my *aenti.*"

Katie's look softened. "*Jah.* I'm Katie Graber. But if those dogs don't leave, I'm going to be late for my first day."

Rachel frowned at her *bruder,* who seemed to be enjoying poor Katie's distress. "Caleb, take her out the back door and get her to your buggy before those dogs come after her again. You'll have to take her to school."

Caleb scowled at his *schweschder.* "What about the leak?"

Rachel shooed him with her hand. "It'll keep until you get back. You can put the bucket back under the sink." Her attention turned to Katie, who looked helplessly shaken from the experience. "She can't be late for her first day. What kind of impression would that make on her students?"

Rachel reached for the books in Katie's hands and set them on the counter. "You will probably want to straighten your hair and fix your *kapp*. It's nearly off your head. I'll get you a few pins to tack the hem of your dress back together."

Caleb sighed in defeat. Rachel had always bossed him around even though she was his younger *schweschder,* but Rachel had an authoritative influence about her that Caleb found tough to match. He went to put the bucket back under the leaky sink and wiped down the grime from his face, hands, and arms. He wasn't sure why he cared what the snobby school teacher thought of him. But she was beautiful and educated, and he didn't want to appear unkempt in her sparkling blue eyes.

CHAPTER 2

Caleb offered his hand to Katie to assist her into his buggy, but she refused, her nose lifted in disdain. He felt self-conscious, wondering if he smelled like the dirty pipes he'd been trying to clean and repair. He didn't know much about the district she'd come from, but he was certain all districts frowned on prideful discord among the people. Maybe she was simply shy. Or she felt uneasy being in strange territory, rather than being snooty, which was his first impression of her.

Once he settled into the seat next to her, he grabbed the reins and clucked to his gelding to urge him out of the snowy rut the wheels had settled in while he'd been at the bakery.

"I'm Caleb. How long will you be teaching here?"

Katie kept her face forward and her chin tipped upward. "I'll be teaching until the end of the school year while my *aenti* recovers from her injuries from her fall. And I caught your name from your new *fraa* at the bakery."

Caleb chuckled. "Rachel is not my *fraa*. She's my younger *schweschder*. I'm not married.*"*

Katie let her eyes drift to Caleb. "You don't look anything alike. And since she seemed to have the upper hand on you, I assumed you were newly married. That, and the lack of beard."

Caleb smiled. "We don't look alike because we have different *mamms*. She can be bossy, but I guess I'm a pushover."

Katie's nose tipped even higher. "That's not a commendable trait for a *mann* to have. I suppose that's probably why you aren't married. A *mann* is supposed to be in charge—be the head of the household."

Caleb smiled. "I'm not married because I haven't found a woman bossy enough to turn my head. I need a strong woman who will keep me in line." His eyes drifted to Katie. "You seem like a strong woman."

Katie sighed with disdain. "I'm not bossy, but perhaps I'm too strong for *you*. But it's no matter because I'm betrothed to Jessup King."

Caleb raised an eyebrow. "Wedding season has just passed. Why didn't you marry then?"

Katie was clearly agitated by his question, but it was obvious he was getting a kick out of irritating her.

"Not that it's any of your concern, but I wasn't ready. I asked for a long engagement."

Caleb chuckled. "Sounds to me like you don't want to marry the *mann.*"

Katie pursed her lips. "That is none of your concern, and I would appreciate it if you would not discuss my personal life."

Caleb's mouth turned up at the corners. "You started it."

Katie turned to him, her brow creased in a deep furrow. Caleb thought she looked even prettier when she was angry.

She glared at him. "Are you twelve?"

Caleb laughed heartily. "I'm twenty-five. How old are you?"

"Not that it's any of your concern, but I'm twenty-three."

Caleb snorted. "That's kind of old not to be married yet."

Katie cleared her throat. "You are one to talk. At least I'm engaged to be married. You don't even appear to have any prospects."

"I told you I haven't found a woman feisty enough to handle me. But you—how long have you been engaged?"

"You're getting awfully personal."

"Are you refusing to answer the question?"

Katie shook her head impatiently. "It's been just over two years."

Caleb muttered under his breath.

Katie leered at him. "What did you say?"

"I just said that I wouldn't wait that long for you."

Katie's face heated with excitement over her handsome driver's forward statement. She suddenly regretted telling him of her parents' arrangement with the King family for her to be married to Jessup. She didn't love him enough to marry him, but her family had called it a *gut* match. Who was she to argue?

At the time, there were no other prospects for her, and it was certainly better than becoming a spinster. But marrying only to avoid becoming a spinster was not a reason to marry. She'd hoped that time would put love in her heart for Jessup, but it hadn't. She knew there was only so much time she could keep the engagement going. Eventually, Jessup would expect to marry her. What then?

Katie couldn't see herself entering into a loveless marriage with the older widower any more than she could see herself as a *mamm* to his two children. She'd tried to break it off with him several times, but he just wouldn't accept it, and neither would her parents. She'd even avoided him for the past two weeks, making excuses to avoid taking buggy rides with him, but he was not one to take no for an answer.

The thought of marriage to a *mann* like Caleb excited her. If only there was a way out of her situation. Perhaps her absence from the community in Nappanee would change Jessup's mind about her—especially since she hadn't even told him she was leaving. She'd prayed about that very thing when she was offered the opportunity to take over teaching for her *aenti*. Was it possible that *Gott* was answering her prayers? Discouragement set in as she thought of her betrothed. There was no way another *mann* would consider her as long as she was promised to Jessup.

Caleb steered the gelding toward the school *haus,* enjoying Katie's company. The fact that she was betrothed bothered him more than it should. After all, they'd just met. But she was just the kind of woman he could see himself marrying.

- If you enjoyed this preview, you may purchase the book in its entirety at the same online retailer you purchased this book.

HAPPY READING

Book Four
Jacob's Daughter series

Coming November, 2012

Made in the USA
San Bernardino, CA
20 February 2014